Language, Gender, and Power

The Politics of Representation and Hegemony
in South Asia

Language, Gender, and Power

The Politics of Representation and Hegemony in South Asia

SHAHID SIDDIQUI

OXFORD

UNIVERSITY PRESS

OXFORD
UNIVERSITY PRESS

Oxford University Press is a department of the University of Oxford.
It furthers the University's objective of excellence in research, scholarship,
and education by publishing worldwide in

Oxford New York

Auckland Cape Town Dar es Salaam Hong Kong Karachi
Kuala Lumpur Madrid Melbourne Mexico City Nairobi
New Delhi Shanghai Taipei Toronto

With offices in

Argentina Austria Brazil Chile Czech Republic France Greece
Guatemala Hungary Italy Japan Poland Portugal Singapore
South Korea Switzerland Turkey Ukraine Vietnam

Published in Pakistan by Oxford University Press

© Oxford University Press 2014

First published 2014

ISBN 978-0-19-906739-8

Typeset in Adobe Garamond Pro
Printed in Pakistan by
Kagzi Printers, Karachi.
Published by
Ameena Saiyid, Oxford University Press
No. 38, Sector 15, Korangi Industrial Area, PO Box 8214,
Karachi-74900, Pakistan.

In memory of
my beloved
MOTHER

Contents

List of Tables   ix
Acknowledgements   xi
Introduction   xiii

Part 1   Language, Representation, and Hegemony

Chapter   1   Language: A Socio-political Phenomenon   2
Chapter   2   Power and Politics of Discourse   8
Chapter   3   Language, Representation, and Control   16

Part 2   Language and Gender Construction

Chapter   4   Manufacturing Gender and Language   28
Chapter   5   Growing Up With Gender   46
Chapter   6   Language and Gender: Research Directions   52

Part 3   Language, Gender, and Society

Chapter   7   Literature and the Politics of Exclusion   62
Chapter   8   Sayings, Proverbs, and Women   77
Chapter   9   Gender and Jokes   85
Chapter 10   Matrimonial Ads: Societal Expectations   100

Part 4   Language, Gender, and Education

Chapter 11   Gender and Education   116
Chapter 12   Nursery Rhymes and Gender Representation   125
Chapter 13   Representation of Women in Fairy Tales   138

PART 5   LANGUAGE, GENDER, AND THE MEDIA

Chapter 14   Gender and Media   156
Chapter 15   Women in Advertisements   162
Chapter 16   Television Plays and Gender Stereotypes   169
Chapter 17   Construction of Gender in Films   176
Chapter 18   Representation of Women in Songs   182

PART 6   GENDERED DISCOURSE: REFORM AND RESISTANCE

Chapter 19   Need for Language Reform   192
Chapter 20   Resistance through Language   198

Bibliography   207
Index   217

List of Tables

4.1   Attributes Assigned to Male and Female   33

4.2   Terms Assigned to Male and Female   33

4.3   Traits Assignable to Male (Instrumental) or   39
      Female (Expressive) Roles

4.4   Pairs of Terms for Males and Females   43

10.1 Married Adolescents: 101
      Percentage of Married 15–19 Year-Olds

10.2 Sample Distribution   107

10.3 Male seeking suitors   108

10.4 Attributes in female ads   109

10.5 Top Five Attributes in Matrimonial Ads in Pakistan   110

10.6 Females seeking suitors in India   112

10.7 Females seeking suitors in Sri Lanka   113

10.8 Top Five Attributes in Female ads in Pakistan,   113
      India, and Sri Lanka

13.1 Average Number of References to Physical   141
      Appearance and Beauty/Handsomeness
      by Character's Gender and Age for All Books

14.1 Representation of Men and Women in Media   158

14.2 Highlighting Issues Concerning Gender in Media   159

14.3 Reinforcing or Challenging Stereotypes   159

14.4 Media Effects on Women   160

19.1 Sexism and Language   194

19.2 Alternative Expression   195

19.3 Alternative Expression   195

Acknowledgements

The process of writing a book is like a journey to a distant land, full of excitements, frustrations, disappointment, distractions, surprises, discoveries, and rewards. For me, this journey, which had started seven years ago, is finally coming to an end. During this long and, at times, tiring journey I was given academic assistance and emotional support by a number of people. Without them, this journey was simply impossible. I take this opportunity to thank all those whose help, cooperation, and encouragement made it happen. I would like to thank Umar, Javaria, Parveen, Sufia, Saeed, and Nasir for their constant support. I would like to thank all my students in various places who were a source of inspiration and learning for me. I would also like to thank Asma, my wife, for her motivation and support.

Introduction

Language had long been considered as a neutral and passive phenomenon whose main function was to communicate or to reflect what was happening in the society. This value-free view of language led to the use of a quantitative approach to the study of language, where different aspects of language, i.e. grammar, phonology, and semantics, were studied in isolation. Especially in South Asian societies, the study of English revolved around learning of grammatical rules and structures. The focus on usage, form, and structure impacted negatively on students' actual use of language.

Language proficiency was thus linked solely with grammatical accuracy and the knowledge of grammatical rules was considered as a major criterion for language proficiency. This apparently very convincing view was challenged by Hymes (1972), who drew our attention to another important aspect of language proficiency, i.e. communicative competence, which was hitherto ignored by the linguists. The notion of communicative competence highlighted the *social* aspect of language.

This active social aspect of language was brought to light in a convincing manner by Sapir and Whorf, whose hypothesis presented language as a constitutive force in the construction of social reality. The hypothesis challenged the value-free view of language and led to the viewpoint that the function of language is not just reflection but it is also involved in the construction and perpetuation of social reality. Although the branch of socio-linguistics was already there, the *socio* part of it was not very active (Romaine, 2000). The general view of linguistics was an 'objective' study of language.

This 'objectivity' in the process of studying linguistics either ignored or underestimated issues of power and politics. Butler (2000: 175) rightly points out that, 'Language is not an *exterior medium of instrument* into which I pour a self and from which I glean a reflection of that self.' There has recently been a growing realization of the relationship of language and power and thus a need to bring forth the critical aspect of applied linguistics for discussion. This critical aspect could only be appreciated if we adopt an interdisciplinary approach to the study of language. This may include benefiting from theories of sociology, psychology, politics, gender studies, anthropology, literature, culture studies, feminism, etc. to obtain a more holistic view of intricate language related issues. Language, in its turn, plays an important part in understanding the concepts contained within these disciplines.

How is language associated with power in the process of hegemony? Gramsci (1996) elaborated the role of the discursive approach in controlling others. Said (1978) demonstrated the role of discourse in constructing social reality and its role in the politics of representation. His work was inspired by the theories of Gramsci and Foucault, who considered discourse to be a highly political phenomenon, directly linked with power. As the linkage of discourse and power was brought forth by certain linguists, anthropologists, and social thinkers, a number of movements, including the feminist movement, realized the importance of language, got inspiration from it and used it for constructing their arguments.

The notion of gender, which is a social construct (explained in detail in Chapters 4 and 5), determines the roles, expectations, and opportunities for women and men. Language plays an important part in the process of socialization. The issue of differences, in the languages spoken by men and women, was taken up by Jesperson (1922), who devoted a chapter entitled *The Woman* in his book, suggesting that women's language is something deviant from the standard, men's language.

But the real focus on the mutual relationship of language and gender came with the arrival of Lakoff's *Language and Woman's Place* (1975) followed by Spender's *Man Made Language,* and Deborah Tannen's *You Just Don't Understand.* These books tried to understand the issue of language and gender from different perspectives. Simone de Beauvoir's *The Second Sex* (1949) and Judith Butler's *Gender Trouble* (1990) provided some useful theoretical bases for this discussion.

One should, however, not forget the role of the feminist movement, which gave impetus to the issue of gender and its relationship with language. It was the feminist critique of language that underscored the issue of power and underlined the significance of the socio-political context. Feminists also shifted the emphasis from the language used *by* women to language used *about* women.

The most interesting aspect of this language and gender linkage is that language helps perform gender (Austin, 1962; Butler, 1990, 1993; Crawford, 1995). Gender is performed every day in different walks of life through different means of expression, e.g., sayings and proverbs, jokes, songs, advertisements, films, theatre, and TV plays, etc.

In South Asian countries, where there has always been a serious challenge of low female literacy rates, the discipline of gender studies is relatively new. Although there were women studies departments functioning in some universities, the questions of power and politics were not pursued in such programmes in an academic manner. It was in 2004, when I planned to offer the course *Language, Gender, and Power* at Lahore University of Management Sciences (LUMS), that I realized the paucity of indigenous academic work in this area.

During the pre-course preparation phase, I travelled to different universities and met with NGO (Non-Governmental Organization) personnel working on issues of gender. I could not find a single course in the universities of Pakistan focusing language and gender with special reference to the question of power. In some universities, there were programmes in the field of women studies but the critical and reflective approach was missing. Some NGOs, including ASR, Simorgh, Uks, and Shirkat Gah, had a positive contribution in creating awareness about gender disparity through research and publications but most of the other NGOs' work suffered from various problems: (a) The material they were using was imported from abroad without personal reflection. (b) An extreme approach against men was adopted. (c) There was inadequate academic depth in their work. (d) The indigenous context was ignored while discussing the issue of gender. (e) There was not much work available on the issue of language and gender.

This book is a result of my intimate involvement with the Language, Gender, and Power course I have been teaching in LUMS and Lahore School of Economics since 2004. Teaching a course on this topic was an exciting and enriching experience for me.

The book is divided into six parts.

Part 1, *Language, Representation, and Hegemony* (Chapters 1–3): This part focuses on language and tries to unpack the issue of power and politics in relation to language. It deals with the issues of language as a political phenomenon, notions of power, politics of discourse, language and control, and construction of social reality and representation.

Part 2, *Language and Gender Construction* (Chapters 4–6): This part focuses on gender and language and deals with the topics of manufacturing of gender, language and gender, and research done in the area of language and gender.

Part 3, *Language and Gender Performance* (Chapters 7–10): This part is based on the indigenous examples of gender construction and gender perpetuation in South Asian societies. It deals with gender construction in the areas of sayings and proverbs, jokes, songs, film, theatre, and literature.

Part 4, *Language, Gender, and Education* (Chapters 11–13): It focuses on formal education for children in schools and their exposure to nursery rhymes and fairy tales.

Part 5, *Language, Gender, and Media* (Chapters 14–18): This part deals with the impact of media, commercial advertisements, television plays, songs, and their role in the construction and perpetuation of gendered stereotypes.

Part 6, *Gendered Discourse: Reform and Resistance* (Chapters 19–20): It deals with the questions of language reforms and resistance through language.

The approach adopted in the book is interdisciplinary in nature. One can trace threads of sociology, linguistics, gender studies, feminism, literature, politics, and anthropology, etc., used in order to have a fuller view of the phenomenon of language and to understand and appreciate the issues of language, gender, and power and their interaction.

The book is not written exclusively on gender or language. Rather, it focuses on the interrelationship of language, gender, and power and their impact on one another. It is an attempt to see gender through language. In other words, the issue of gender is viewed from the perspective of language. Being of an interdisciplinary nature, this book should interest academics, students, researchers, curriculum planners, and policy makers in the fields of gender studies, linguistics, sociology, politics, and culture studies. The book should also interest the members of civil society as it deals with social change in terms of reducing gender gaps by being more sensitive to language use.

PART 1

LANGUAGE, REPRESENTATION, AND HEGEMONY

Chapter 1
Language: A Socio-political Phenomenon

Everyone lives in a given language; everyone's experiences therefore are had, absorbed, and recalled in that language.

– Edward Said

Ideologies are closely linked to language, because using language is the commonest form of social behaviour, and the form of social behaviour where we rely on 'common-sense' assumptions.

– Norman Fairclough

Only a few decades ago the popular paradigm, prevalent in most of the educational institutions in South Asia, was highly positivistic in nature. In this paradigm, language was considered a purely linguistic phenomenon, comprising semantics, phonology, and grammar. The study of language was usually done on an *etherised table* in a lab-like controlled environment, where linguists would dissect it into different components and analyse them in isolation. Sweeping judgements were passed about languages, e.g., X was a superior language or Y was an inferior language, etc. This fixed and judgemental view of language was a natural consequence of studying it in isolation.

LANGUE AND PAROLE

It was Saussure, cited by Fairclough (2001: 5) who introduced two useful terms *langue* and *parole* to describe the two aspects of language and reinterpret the phenomenon of language. *Langue* denotes the rules and regulations and *parole* refers to the actual use of language. This division of *usage* and *use* encouraged other linguists to explore the socio-cultural dimensions of language.

A gradual realization started taking place that language has a strong link with its speakers and no language, in its essence, is strong or weak but it is the group of speakers of a particular language that decides its strength. A very recent example is the status of Persian in the Indian subcontinent. Persian was considered to be a symbol of prestige and status but, after the decline of the Mughal empire and the ascendance of the British in the subcontinent, Persian was gradually replaced by other local languages and English began to emerge as a language of power and prestige. It was not because of the innate strength of the English language but because of the powerful group of speakers who owned it that English attained a prestigious status.

LANGUAGE AND SOCIETY

Since the speakers of a language live in a certain society, it is important that the study of language take into account its linkage with society. Not long ago, proficiency in the English language was largely linked with accuracy, i.e. grammatical use of language. It was Hymes (1972) who advocated the idea of communicative competence. According to this notion, grammatical accuracy alone was not sufficient for language proficiency; social appropriateness was also required. The notion of social appropriateness highlights the significance of context and the legitimacy of some basic questions like: What is the topic of conversation? Who are you? Who are you speaking to? What is your relationship with him/her? Why are you engaged in communication? Where is this communication taking place? When is this conversation taking place? The answers to these questions can help produce a socially appropriate discourse.

LANGUAGE AS A SOCIAL PHENOMENON

Fairclough (2001: 19) explores a deeper level linkage between language and society. According to him:

> . . . there is not an external relationship 'between' language and society, but an internal and dialectical relationship. Language is a part of society; linguistic phenomena *are* social phenomena of a special sort, and social phenomena *are* (in part) linguistic phenomena.

It is interesting to observe how society impacts and shapes a language and how certain sociological factors influence our choice and use of words (Trudgill, 1983; Romaine, 2000). Some of these sociological factors are age, social class, social relationship, gender, religion, education, and ethnicity. So, in most of the cases, we can have a fair idea of the identity of people by listening to their language. Similarly, geographical surroundings also impact the number and frequency of words for something which is common and central to that setting. For instance, in Eskimo language, there are many words for snow, as there is a large number of words for the camel in the Arabic language. The examples stated so far reflect the unidirectional relationship, i.e. how a society impacts language. This direction of relationship is easy to understand because of our day to day observations. It presents language as a passive phenomenon, where language is no more than a tool of communication or reflection.

CHANGING PERCEPTIONS OF LANGUAGE

It was in 1929 that Sapir came up with a hypothesis which was to revolutionize the study of language. According to Sapir, quoted in Burke and Crowley (2000: 397):

> Human beings do not live in the objective world alone, nor alone in the world of social activity as ordinarily understood, but are very much at the mercy of the particular language which has become the medium

of expression for their society. It is quite an illusion to imagine that one adjusts to reality essentially without the use of language and that language is merely an incidental means of solving specific problems of communication or reflection. The fact of the matter is that the 'real world' is to a large extent unconsciously built upon the language habits of the group. No two languages are ever sufficiently similar to be considered as representing the same social reality. The worlds in which different societies live are distinct worlds, not merely the same world with different labels attached.

This statement challenged the conservative view of language and redetermined its traditional function of language—reflection of outer facts—and emphasised that language is also involved in the *construction* of the outer world. Whorf, quoted by Carroll (2008: 396) suggests:

We dissect nature along lines laid down by our native languages. The categories and types that we isolate from the world of phenomena we do not find there because they stare every observer in the face; on the contrary, the world is presented in a kaleidoscopic flux of impressions which has to be organized by our minds—and this means largely by the linguistic systems in our minds.

According to this hypothesis, we perceive the outer world with the help of our language.

IMPACT OF LANGUAGE ON SOCIETY

The Sapir-Whorf hypothesis helps us appreciate language from a different perspective, i.e. it is not just society that impacts language, but language also influences society. The function of language is thus not just to reflect what is happening in life; it is also involved in the construction of social reality. Wykes and Gunter (2005: 61) suggest that, 'Language is both a vital part of how we interact with others and the world but also the means by which we know ourselves and our world through the mental concepts enabled by language.' This direction of relationship, i.e. the impact of language on society, is quite subtle and consequently not easily apparent to observation. The two-way relationship of language and society suggests that language is not a neutral and passive entity but a highly political, social, and cultural phenomenon.

DENOTATION AND CONNOTATION

Each word has a literal meaning and a connotative meaning, which is a kind of associated meaning constructed by society. In turn, these words constitute a certain kind of social reality. Adeniyi (2000: para 8) gives a list of some words and expressions which are politically loaded. For example:

> . . . western world, hard currency, developing world, terrorists, hard-liner, moderate, reform, secular, portico, single parent, sexual orientation, white people, black people, yellow people, red people, first world, third world, anti-Semitism, free market economy, bribery and corruption, tribe, ethnic, leprosy or Hanson's disease, fat and full bodied, accent, international community, weapons of mass destruction and so on and so forth.

Just by reading these words and expressions, one accesses instant perceptions which are socially constructed, mainly by the dominant groups.

Gramsci (1996) discusses the notion of hegemony by referring to two approaches which may be used to attain hegemony or control: a *coercive* approach, which is associated with political society, and a *discursive* approach, which is linked with civil society and thrives on social institutions. According to Gramsci, the discursive approach is more effective. As discourse is essentially made up of language, language is actively involved in the process of control and may act as a tool of hegemony. A society is intellectually dominated by certain stereotypes, which are made up and perpetuated by language. This suggests the active political role language can play in the dynamics of power.

INTERNATIONAL POLITICAL DISCOURSE

The examples of political discourse can be seen on national and international scenes as well, where certain stereotypes and labels have been constructed, advocated, and popularized. Let us look at an interesting example, quoted by Chomsky in his book, *Language and Politics* (2004a: 542). He notes that the USA used to have a 'War Department' until 1947. Since then, the name of this department has been changed to 'Defense Department'. A little twist in language makes the same department more acceptable. Language that is used to represent, much of the time misrepresents the facts.

LANGUAGE AND RESISTANCE

It is important to note that language can also be used to put up resistance. One way of doing it, according to Foucault, is through reversal of discourse. Foucault (1995) is of the opinion that powerful and powerless are not fixed positions. Once powerful may become powerless and once powerless may become powerful at another point in history. To him the distinguishing factor between powerful and powerless is discourse, for which a constant struggle is going on. Marginalised groups need to realize the central significance of discourse as a potential tool to shift the advantage in their favour. We shall discuss this topic in detail in Chapter 20 of this book.

Chapter 2
Power and Politics of Discourse

. . . power is everywhere not because it embraces everything, but because it comes from everywhere.

– Michel Foucault

[Discourse is] a social practice [which] implies a dialectal relationship between a particular discursive event and situation(s), institution(s) and social structure(s) which frame it. A dialectal relationship is a two way relationship: the discursive event is shaped by situations, institutions, social structures, but it is also shaped by them.

– Fairclough and Wodak

Power, being a complex concept, can be defined in different ways. One common attribute in different definitions is that of 'control'. Most of the time power is considered as the ability or right to control people or events. If we look at the history of human beings, we see people using the tool of violence to demonstrate their power to control others. There was a time when large fighting forces and deadly weapons were considered as important conditions of power. We then see a change as the focus shifts from large army size to more sophisticated weapons systems, espionage equipment, and computerized weaponry. The urge, however, remains the same, controlling others by demonstrating power.

DISCURSIVE POWER

For a long time the terms 'control' and 'hegemony' were associated with coercion, i.e. use of force. Antonio Gramsci offers another view of hegemony in his seminal *Prison Notebooks,* written during 1929–35 in jail. Gramsci refers to two approaches to hegemony. One is through spontaneous consent, in which general directions are imposed by dominant groups on social life. According to Gramsci (1996: 12), consent is 'caused by the prestige (and consequent confidence) which the dominant group enjoys because of its position and function in the world of production'. The second approach to hegemony, according to Gramsci (1996: 12), is through the 'apparatus of state coercive power which "legally" enforces discipline on those groups who do not "consent" either actively or passively.' Hegemony through spontaneous consent is a clear reference to the discursive approach to hegemony, which appears to be more effective than the coercive approach.

POWER AS INFLUENCE

The discursive approach draws our attention to another defining attribute of power, i.e. influence. Polsby, cited in Lukes (2005: 17–18), suggests:

> One can conceive of 'power'—'influence' and 'control' are serviceable synonyms—as the capacity of one actor to do something affecting another actor, which changes the probable pattern of specified future events. This can be envisaged most easily in a decision-making situation.

We can see power as an ability to influence other people's choices, behaviours, and acts. Coercive power is usually used by the state 'legally' by exercising the authority vested in it. This suggests that 'authority' is a legalized version of 'power'. Lukes (2005) discusses three dimensions of power. The first two dimensions refer to decision-making and agenda setting. The third dimension deals with shaping ideologies, perception, and norms. Referring to the third dimension of power, Lukes (2005: 28) suggests:

. . . is it not the supreme and most insidious exercise of power to prevent people, to whatever degree, from having grievances by shaping their perceptions, cognitions and preferences in such a way that they accept their role in the existing order of things, either because they can see or imagine no alternative to it, or because they see it as natural and unchangeable, or because they value it as divinely ordained and beneficial?

This dimension of power is closer to what Gramsci describes as spontaneous consent.

KNOWLEDGE AND POWER

Foucault also delves into the issue of power. Gauntlett (2003: 117) notes that:

> For Foucault, power is not an asset which a person can *have*; rather, power is something *exercised* within interactions. Power *flows through* relationships, or networks of relationships. You couldn't really say that someone was powerful, per se, then; but you could say that they frequently found themselves in a powerful position, or had many opportunities to exercise power.

In fact, his search started with tracing the history of knowledge, when he realized the strong linkage between knowledge and power. Foucault discovered that, with new knowledge and technologies, new manifestations of power and control are invented. Instead of using the traditional violent power and destroying the opponent altogether, modern technologies have different strategies of control. In *Discipline and Punish*, Foucault (1995: 138) describes the contemporary version of power,

> . . . it defined how one may have a hold over others' bodies, not only so that they may do what one wishes, but so that may operate as one wishes, with the techniques, the speed and the efficiency that one

determines. Thus discipline produces subjected and practiced bodies, 'docile' bodies.

These techniques of knowledge and power were initially used in isolated institutions like prisons, factories, and schools, etc., but later on they were used in other contexts as well.

TRANSITORY NATURE OF POWER

The role of discourse is crucial in the formation of knowledge. It is the discursive formation of objects that can construct certain kind of knowledge that leads to new techniques of power and control. Power, by contemporary thinkers, is not viewed as a product but as a process, which means that it is not fixed or located in place; it is transitory, fluid, and relational in nature. Power, as Foucault puts it, is relational, which is structured by discourse. This suggests that the relationship between the powerful and the powerless is not fixed and permanent. This has a direct implication for the possibility of resistance.

LANGUAGE AND CONSTRUCTION OF REALITY

As discussed in Chapter 1, the Sapir-Whorf hypothesis challenged the stereotypical belief that language is a passive and neutral tool. It put forward the thesis that language itself is involved in the construction of social reality. This thesis also suggested that the function of language is not just reflection or communication of what is happening outside but language also performs two other important functions, i.e. the construction of social reality and its perpetuation (Chapter 1). This central position of language, in terms of construction of social reality, raises some important questions. These questions include: What is discourse? What is the interrelationship of discourse and social order? How is discourse linked with power and politics? How is it engaged in construction

.of social reality? How is it used to hegemonize the marginalised groups? How can discourse be used to put up resistance?

DEFINING DISCOURSE

In order to address these questions, we need to unpack the term 'discourse'. According to Sunderland (2006: 47), 'Discourse has a variety of meanings, varying with discipline and intellectual persuasion. Linguistic meanings include the broad 'stretch of written or spoken language', and the more specific 'linguistic, and accompanying paralinguistic, interaction between people in a specific context' (Talbot 1995a: 45). The debate on discourse came into spotlight with the work of the French social thinker Michel Foucault, whose notion of knowledge and power relies heavily on discourse. The term discourse, like many other elusive terms, can be interpreted at different levels. One oversimplified definition of discourse describes it as 'written or oral text'. But this definition, which presents language as something neutral, is incomplete and misleading. Discourse acquired new meanings when Foucault propounded his famous theory of knowledge and power.

LANGUAGE AND SOCIAL PRACTICE

The term 'discourse' came into focus again in the work of Norman Fairclough, who pioneered and popularized Critical Discourse Analysis (CDA). Fairclough (2001: 14) suggests that discourse means 'language as social practice determined by social structures'. According to Fairclough, cited in Atanga (2010: 26), discourse is: 'Ways of representing aspects of the world—the processes, relations and structures of the material world, the "mental world" of thoughts, feelings, beliefs and so forth, and the social world.' This new interpretation of discourse by Fairclough helped others to revisit this term, realise its significant role in the construction of social reality and view it as a socio-political phenomenon. One can now find a more holistic definition of discourse in dictionaries. For instance, Merriam-Webster dictionary (http://www.merriam-webster.com) defines discourse as 'a mode of organizing knowledge, ideas, or experience that is rooted in language and its concrete contexts (as history or institutions).' According to Fairclough (2001: 20), discourse involves 'social conditions which can be specified as *social conditions of production*, and *social conditions of interpretations.*'

In almost all imperialistic adventures, language is used as a potent tool of control. It is important to note how the discourses of the powerful become the model to follow and act as standards for others. Anyone deviating from these standards is dubbed as 'sub-standard'. All this is done in an ostensibly 'objective' manner. The dominant groups make use of the discursive approach to hegemonize marginalised groups. A detailed discussion on this topic can be read in Said's *Orientalism* (1978) and Phillipson's, *Linguistic Imperialism* (1992).

Discourse, Knowledge, and Power

Foucault identifies a nexus of power, discourse, and knowledge. The relationship of power and knowledge is important to understand. Power generally has a hold on the requisite sources (grip on the institutions) for creating the required discourses to construct the targeted social realities. The constructed knowledge/social reality rendered by discourse justifies all the actions of the powerful and condemns those who do not comply with them. With the help of discourse, the dominant groups represent the marginalised groups with their biases. Certain desired 'truths', 'facts', and 'ideologies' are constructed with the help of discourse and people, ideas, and objects are evaluated and judged in the light of these.

POWER AND RESISTANCE

Foucault, as cited by Sugden and Tomlinson (2002: 7), makes a reference to the points of resistance available in the dynamics of power. The relational character of power is such that 'their existence depends on a multiplicity of points of resistance: these play the role of adversary, target, support, or handle in power relations. These points of resistance are present everywhere in the power network.'

This view of power is optimistic in nature as it does not lump power in one location and view it as a static object. On the contrary, it looks at power as something scattered around us in different networks. There is a constant struggle between power and its adversary and there are points of resistance available within the process of power for the act of resistance.

DISCOURSE AND RESISTANCE

It is important that, in our school curricula, we include the critical study of language that exposes students to the socio-political use of language. This exposure is crucial as Candlin (1989: ix) suggests that, 'an understanding of the social order is most conveniently and naturally achieved through a critical awareness of the power of language.' The need to study language from a critical perspective is also underlined by Pennycook (1994, 2001). Understanding the dynamics of power, discourse, and knowledge is a prerequisite for the use of language for putting up resistance. The proponents of critical discourse analysis consider it as an effective means to discern the hegemonic discursive strategies. Wodak (1997: 7) suggests that, 'Critical discourse analysis, in my view, is an instrument whose purpose is precisely to expose power structures and "disorders of discourse".'

REVERSAL OF DISCOURSE

The balance of power can be disturbed by reversing the discourse. We have seen such examples of discourse reversal in the feminist movement. The reversal of discourse, on the one hand, challenges created truths, facts, common sense, and ideologies, and, on the other hand, offers alternative truths and facts. Canagarajah, (1999: 30) suggests that, '*Discourse* is the linguistic realization of the social construct *ideology*.' Thus, if we wish to use literacy and language for emancipation, freedom, and development, we need to challenge some of the stereotypes, commonsense social practices, and ideologies. This can only be done with the help of a critical insight of the potential role of language in creating, maintaining, and challenging hegemonic practices.

Chapter 3
Language, Representation, and Control

> . . . ideas, cultures, and histories cannot seriously be understood or studied without their force, or more precisely their configurations of power. . . .
>
> – Edward Said

> . . . what we assume to be background knowledge or common sense in fact are always ideological representations; that is to say, what we assume to be common everyday knowledge is in fact always the particular worldview (ideology) of a particular social group.
>
> – Alastair Pennycook

In the process of studying the configuration of power, we come to realize the inevitable role of language. The relationship of language with power and politics has been discussed by linguists and political thinkers in the past. More recently, there have been attempts to study language in relation to psychology, sociology, anthropology, politics, philosophy, development, and gender studies. This interdisciplinary approach has led to critical explorations of the links between language, politics, and power. Pennycook's book, *Critical Applied Linguistics* (2001) makes a solid case for bringing forth the sociopolitical view of language and stresses the need to study language with a critical perspective.

LANGUAGE AND COMMUNICATION

The language-thought debate goes back to the times of the Greek scholars. The thinkers were divided into two schools of thought:

one considered language as merely the dress of thought and the other viewed it as a mould that had the capability to change the shape of thought. The common notion about language was that of a relatively passive tool for communication.

The socio-cultural aspect of language was viewed from a political perspective by Gramsci (1996), when he referred to the significant role of civil society and social institutions. How could language be linked with hegemony? How the discursive approach is more effective than the coercive approach? These central questions were later picked up by Foucault as he came up with a new meaning for the term 'discourse'. Discourse and its link with power were elaborated by Foucault in his works *Archaeology of Knowledge* and *Discipline and Punish*.

LANGUAGE AND REPRESENTATION

A slight change in discourse during the process of representation can bring a change in meaning. How language can play a vital part in the process of *representation* has been aptly demonstrated by Said in his book *Orientalism,* where the *Occident* represents the *Orient* with all its biases. This construction of the Orient, according to Said (1978: 8), was made possible, 'Not simply by empirical reality but by a battery of desire, repression, investments, and projections.' The discourse that represents the *Orient* emanates from a certain kind of 'flexible positional superiority', as Said would call it.

MANUFACTURING OF CONSENT

It is important to understand that language plays an important part in representation and the construction of a tunnel vision for readers/listeners/viewers. Some of the strategies of social construction are discussed by Said (1978: 3) when he talks about the construction of the *Orient* by the *Occident* by, '. . . dealing with it by making statements about it, authorizing views of it, describing it, by teaching it, settling it, ruling over it. . . .'

CONSTRUCTION OF CONSENT

Besides Said, Chomsky also discussed the process of social construction at length in many of his writings, in general, and in *Media and Control* in particular, where he discusses the lethal weapon of propaganda that is largely constructed with the help of language. Chomsky coins the terms 'engineering opinion' and 'manufacturing consent' which, according to him (2004b: 14–15), mean 'to bring about agreement on the part of the public for things that they didn't want by the new techniques of propaganda.' The 'manufacturing of consent' is conveniently brought about by the choice and use of certain vocabulary in a persuasive manner by using modern technological means. This manufacturing of consent has its thematic linkage with Gramsci's notion of 'spontaneous consent' where the target group mentally surrenders to the hegemony of the dominant group with its 'free will'.

CONSTRUCTING REPRESENTATION

Having looked at the role of language in representation of objects, ideas, and people let us consider the dynamics of constructing representation. It is important to note that the dominant, powerful, and hegemonic groups have the privilege of representing the subdued, weak, and marginalized groups. Power and discourse have an interesting relationship; they justify and legitimize each other. The dominant groups, being at a vantage position, paint the marginalised groups in their own favourite colours. These constructed representations, with their excessive use and legitimization through various social institutions, become 'convincing reality' in that society. These engineered *facts* and *realities* are internalized by the target groups who start believing in them. This is also applicable to gendered discourses and practices that impact and shape the identities. Eckert and McConnell-Ginet (2003: 305) maintain that, 'Gender is a set of practices through which people construct and claim identities, not simply a system for categorizing people. And gender practices are not only about establishing identities but also about managing social relations.'

USING THE VOCABULARY OF MEN

As we see, in the case of a number of assertiveness courses, women were encouraged to choose and use the vocabulary of men. Goddard and Patterson (2000: 75) refer to this situation: . . . 'women have been forced to use a language which is not their own and which they therefore cannot use to express their experiences effectively: in other words, they have been forced to see the world through male eyes. This is because women have been excluded historically from the production of powerful public discourses.' Hussain (1994: 108) comments on the representation of women by men as:

> To be the object of another's discourse is to suffer an erasure, for representation can only be of that which is not there. The real is displaced by the image, the signified by the signifier. As a result the recognition of the object is based on the connotation or meaning conveyed by and inherent in the signifier.

MEN ARE THE NORM

The logic behind emulating men is that their acts have been propagated as norms and standards. Beauvoir (1997: 15), commenting about the asymmetrical relations between men and women, writes:

> A man is in the right in being a man; it is the woman who is in the wrong. It amounts to this: just as for the ancients there was an absolute

vertical with reference to which the oblique was defined, so there is an absolute human type, the masculine.

In the age of technologically advanced print and electronic media, the politics of *representation* has become much more pervasive in terms of its access to a large audience belonging to a wide range of geographical regions and its instant impact on the target groups.

LANGUAGE AND CONTROL

According to Renzetti and Curran (2002: 138), 'The power of words lies in the fact that the members of a culture share those meanings and valuations. It is their common language that allows the members of a society to communicate and understand one another, and thus makes for order in the society.' It is this aspect of language that tempted the forces of domination to use it as a tool of control. For instance, almost all the major colonial powers exploited language as a weapon of hegemony. This role of language became more prominent in the neo-colonial period. To understand the desire and technique of controlling groups of people and countries, the Gramscian notion of hegemony is useful. Gramsci (1996: 12) refers to two super structural 'levels', i.e. 'civil society' and 'political society'. Civil society refers to 'the private' and political society refers to 'the State'. These, two levels, according to Gramsci (1996: 12) '. . . correspond on the one hand to the function of "hegemony", which the dominant group exercises throughout society, and on the other hand to that of "direct domination" or command exercised through the State and "Juridical" government.'

LANGUAGE AND DOMINANCE

The dominant groups almost always make use of language and culture for hegemonic purposes. It was Phillipson (1992) who raised certain important questions about the dominance of the English language. Phillipson (1992: 47) claims that, '. . . the dominance of English is asserted and maintained by the establishment and continuous reconstitution of structural and cultural inequalities between English and other languages.' The language *inequalities* are advocated and promoted in a systematic manner. A very common strategy that is used by imperialism is to glorify their own language and culture considering them as symbols of *high civilization*. In fact, a number of countries were annexed for the 'noble intention' of civilizing them through superior culture and language.

LANGUAGE AS A TOOL OF HEGEMONY

In India, the East India Company came for trade but as economics and politics go hand in hand, slowly it took over India and a long period of control began in the subcontinent. Besides other techniques of control, the English language was introduced for its *civilizing effect* on the natives. The 1832 Parliamentary Report on language and employment reproduced in Rahman (2004: 10) recommended that, '. . . the general cultivation of the English Language is most highly desirable, both with a view to the introduction of the Natives into Places of Trust, and as a powerful means of operating favourably on their Habits and Character . . .'. It is interesting to note that English was viewed as a means of 'operating favourably on the habits and character of the native people.' In other words, English was presented as essentially a virtuous language that would have positive cultural effects on the local people.

THE MELTING POT APPROACH

As discussed in Chapter 1, no language is inherently weak or strong; it is the socio-political status of the speakers of a certain language that determines its status. Nevertheless, all dominant groups make it a point to glorify their own language and stigmatize the language of *the others*. This *melting pot approach* is common among all dominant powers. This approach recommends all other marginalised cultures to leave their identity and become one with the superior culture of the dominant group. Cohn (1996: 34) refers to Edward Haley, author of the first grammar of the Moors, who found it impossible to discharge his duties without the knowledge of the '*corrupt dialect*'. The tone of Haley suggests a lot when he talks about the local language which, according to him, is not merely a *dialect* but a *corrupt dialect*. Spenser, cited in Burke et al. (2000: 1), points the strategy of colonizers regarding language, '. . . it hath ever been the use of the conqueror to despise the language of the conquered, and to force him by all means to use his'.

GLORIFICATION OF ENGLISH

English was presented in the Indian subcontinent as a supreme language that carried *matchless wisdom*. The judgemental tone and finality of style is evident in Macaulay's *Minute*, written in 1835, where he tried to make a comparison of English with Sanskrit and Arabic. It is important to note that two major communities, i.e. Hindus and Muslims living in India, had passionate affiliations with Sanskrit and Arabic for religious reasons. So it was important to target these two languages. Macaulay, cited by Rahman (2004: 78), did this by ridiculing these languages. '. . . a single shelf of a good European library was worth the whole native literature in India and Arabia.' This sweeping statement came from a person holding an important official portfolio. The lighter side of this issue, however, is that the first line of this paragraph of Macaulay's Minute reads as, 'I have no knowledge of either Sanskrit or Arabic.' This sentence raises serious questions about the validity of Macaulay's claim.

IMPERIALISM AND EDUCATION

The *Minute* by Macaulay underlines the proposed educational system for India and the English language was an integral part of it. The imperialist vision of education is reflected in Macaulay's Minute on Education, cited by Rahman (2004: 88):

> We must at present do our best to form a class who may be interpreters between us and the millions whom we govern; a class of persons, Indians in blood and colour, but English in taste, in opinions, in morals, and in intellect.

Besides Arabic and Sanskrit, which had religious significance in the lives of Muslims and Hindus, Persian was the most potent language of the subcontinent. Persian was dealt with by the colonizers in a systematic manner until it became an abandoned language at official level. Systematically and gradually, funds were appropriated for the promotion of English, and certain perks were attached to it. In government jobs, preference was given to those who were well versed in English. Thus, English was not only a licence for a job in government offices but also a symbol of social status.

TEACHING FOR SUBJUGATION

The foremost purpose of teaching English to the colonized was to create a class of people who could follow instructions and implement the imperialist design. Phillipson (1992: 109) quotes an interesting excerpt from Daniel Defoe's novel, *Robinson Crusoe*. Reading this, ostensibly non-political, work of fiction one can see its political implications. The narrator of the story, who emerges as a symbol of imperialism, talks about the native boy Friday, whom he met on an abandoned island after the shipwreck,

I was greatly delighted with my new companion, and made it my business to teach him everything that was proper to make him useful, handy, and helpful; but especially to make him speak, and understand me when I spake, and he was the aptest scholar that ever was.

Reading this passage carefully, one can see that Friday, the native boy, was given education to make him *useful, handy,* and *helpful* for his master. The boy was taught to speak in order to *understand his master.*

Myths of English Language Teaching

The politics of teaching English still thrives on certain myths. Phillipson (1992: 185) refers to some of them. For instance:

- English is best taught monolingually.
- The ideal teacher of English is a native speaker.
- The earlier English is taught, the better the result.
- The more English is taught, the better the results.
- If other languages are used much, standards of English will drop.

All these myths are promoted deliberately for hegemonic purposes.

Intention vs Presentation

Chomsky (2004a: 541), in *Language and Politics*, talks about the term 'national interest' and suggests that if a political leader says that 'I'm doing this in the national interest', it is 'what's in the interests of small dominant elites who happen to be able to command the resources that enable them to control. . . .'

These examples show the powerful role language can play in construction of social reality and representation of certain 'facts' with vested biases. Schultz (1990: 144) suggests that, '. . . words which are highly charged with emotion, taboo, or distasteful, do not only reflect the culture which uses them. They teach and perpetuate the attitudes which created them.' The position of dominant groups legitimizes a certain discourse which in return validates the action of powerful groups.

PART 2

LANGUAGE AND GENDER CONSTRUCTION

Chapter 4
Manufacturing Gender and Language

Gender is the repeated stylization of the body, a set of repeated acts within a highly rigid regulatory frame which congeal over time to produce the appearance of substance, of a 'natural' kind of being.
— Judith Butler

. . . language and gender are fundamentally embedded in social practice, deriving their meaning from the human activities in which they figure.
— Eckert and McConnell-Ginet

In the previous chapters, we discussed the relationship of language and power. Since language is instrumental in constituting social realities, dominant groups make use of this tool to exercise control over other groups. Bergvall (1999: 274) suggests that most studies of language and gender try to study 'WHETHER there is gender differentiation of language use, WHENCE it arises, WHAT FORMS it takes linguistically, and WHAT EFFECTS it has in society.' This chapter focuses on how gender is socially constructed largely through language, which plays an important role in constructing certain stereotypes. According to Goddard and Patterson (2000: 103), 'Gender does not exist in isolation from factors such as ethnic origin, social class, sexuality or age, and the same "gender" template is likely to fit across these variations only with some fairly drastic distortions.'

THE SECOND SEX

Simone de Beauvoir's seminal book, *The Second Sex,* analysed the gender differences from biological, psychological, historical, and master-slave perspectives. The book raised some pertinent questions and offered some useful insights for further explorations. At the very outset, Beauvoir offers the thesis that, 'Women are not born, they are made.' This makes a direct allusion to the fact that there is a difference between *sex* and *gender*. Sex is a biological division, which is fixed. What is gender then? And how is gender manufactured by sociological, cultural, and political forces? I would like to focus here on this process which has some overt and covert aspects that need to be unpacked in order to understand the phenomenon and its construction.

SEX AND GENDER

Gender in simple terms is a societal view of sex and is variable across time and space. Eckert & McConnell-Ginet (2003: 10) distinguish the two terms by suggesting that, 'Sex is a biological categorization based primarily on reproductive potential, whereas gender is the social elaboration of biological sex.' Goddard and Patterson (2000: 2) make clear distinctions between the terms 'sex' and 'gender' by suggesting that, '"Gender" as a term differs from "sex" in being about socially expected characteristics rather than biology. So, for instance, while processing different genitalia is about biological factors, seeing this as leading to a certain form of behaviour is about gender.' Even the term 'sex' is not apolitical. According to Bergvall and Bing (1996: 3), 'Like gender, sex is socially constructed and better described as a continuum rather than a dichotomy.'

SOME CENTRAL QUESTIONS

How does this social elaboration take place? What is its impact on social relationships? These questions are worth exploring. Before asking these questions, however, let us look at *sex* and *gender* from another angle. Crawford (1995: 15) invites our attention to the central issue in the gender discussion by suggesting that, 'Gender is assumed to be dichotomous—a person can be classified as either "masculine" or "feminine" but not both—and to reside within the individual. Moreover, the masculine pole of this constructed dichotomy is the more valued.' According to Giddens (2006: 458):

> . . . sociologists use the term *sex* to refer to the anatomical and physiological differences that define male and female bodies. *Gender,* by contrast, concerns the psychological, social and cultural differences between males and females. Gender is linked to socially constructed notions of masculinity and femininity; it is not necessarily a direct product of an individual's biological sex.

SOCIALIZATION AND SOCIAL KNOWLEDGE

What makes us perform the way we perform? How do we construct our notion of gender? What makes a certain attitude 'natural' and another 'deviant'? What is the role of language in the construction of stereotypes? Let us try to answer these questions one by one. What we learn from society in the form of culture is learnt or acquired knowledge. The subtle difference between learning and acquisition is that learning involves conscious efforts but in case of acquisition one learns even without making conscious efforts. In the case of social knowledge, both the processes of learning and acquisition are active. The process of social knowledge owes a lot to the process of socialization, where certain social institutions, e.g., family, school, religion, and judiciary, etc., play a very important part. The initial socialization starts at home. It is here that the early concepts are formed. Millet (1969: 33) suggests that, 'Patriarchy's chief institution is the family. It is both a mirror of and a connection with the larger society; a patriarchal unit within a patriarchal whole.'

MEDIA AS A SOCIAL INSTITUTION

A more potent and effective social institution is information media, whether print or electronic, which has emerged as a powerful and swift source of dissemination of social knowledge. This social knowledge, based on certain stereotypes, becomes more imposing through the excessive use of these stereotypes and the legitimization process of the social institutions, including media. Goddard and Patterson (2000: 57) maintain that, 'Stereotyping is very much about the process of applying a simplified model to a real, complex individual, often to negative and derogatory effect.' The conditioning, as a result of excessive use of stereotypes, makes it 'natural' to us and we do not need any other reason or logic to accept the given social knowledge. On similar grounds, we believe in the gendered stereotypes. Eckert and McConnell-Ginet (2003: 9) suggest, 'Gender is embedded so thoroughly in our institutions, our actions, our beliefs, and our desires, that it appears to us to be completely natural.'

STANDARD VS. DEVIANT

The politics of categorization always favours the powerful. This division is so obvious in Gray's book, *Men are from Mars, Women are from Venus*. Talking about men, whom he terms as *Martians*, Gray (1993: 16) observes: 'Martians value power, competency, efficiency, and achievement. They are always doing things to prove themselves and develop their power and skills. Their sense of self is defined through their ability to achieve results. They experience fulfilment primarily through success and accomplishment.' Now let us see how Gray (1993: 18) describes women, whom he calls *Venusians*, 'Venusians have different values. They value love, communication, beauty, and relationships. They spend a lot of time supporting, helping, and nurturing one another. Their sense of self is defined through their feelings and the quality of their relationships. They experience fulfilment through sharing and relating.'

The binary system at work talks about day and night, strong and weak, and high and low. As far as such categories are concerned, there is no apparent harm in talking about the differences, but the problem begins when one is considered good and other as bad, e.g., good/bad, normal/abnormal, standard/deviant, and natural/weird, etc. This kind of labelling has its own politics where certain dominant groups in a society set the *standards* and other groups are marginalized as they do not come up to the set standards.

BIASED REPRESENTATION OF WOMEN

Miller and Swift, quoted by Goddard and Patterson (2000: 75), refer to the biased representation of women in the following areas:

- describing women by appearance, but men by achievement;
- describing women by their relationship to men, but not describing men by their relationship to women;
- referring to women as 'girls' but giving male figures the adult label, 'men';
- using fixed collocations where male referents occur first—as in 'he or she', 'husband and wife', 'men and women'.

Beauvoir (1997: 17) explores the historical development of negative connotation of the feminine element in binary division:

The feminine element was at first no more involved in such pairs as Varuna-Mitra, Uranus-Zeus, Sun-Moon, and Day-Night than it was in the contrast between Good and Evil, lucky and unlucky auspices, right and left, God and Lucifer. Otherness is a fundamental category of human thought.

MALE AND FEMALE: BINARY DIVISION

The binary division of male and female is so rigid that males and females are supposed to possess the attributes of their respective groups.

Table 4.1: Attributes Assigned to Male and Female

Male	Female
Strong	Weak
Brave	Cowardly
Independent	Dependent
Stable	Emotional
Smart	Dumb
Steadfast	Capricious
Composed	Nervous
Extrovert	Introvert
Innovative	Conservative

BIASED REPRESENTATION

Sunderland (2006: 244) points out how language is biased against women by giving some interesting examples of terms used for men and women:

Table 4.2: Terms Assigned to Male and Female

Male term	Connotation	Female term	Connotation
Wizard	Positive	Witch	Negative
Bachelor		Spinster	
Manager	Superior	Manageress	Inferior
Governor		Governess	
Lord		Madam	
Master	No Sexual Connotation	Mistress	Sexual Connotation
King		Queen	
Sir		Lady	

POLITICS OF EVALUATION

Weaver-Hightower (2003: 471) suggests that in every society 'women as a group relative to men are disadvantaged socially, culturally, politically, and economically.' As these discriminatory practices have been there for ages, they appear as *natural* and constitute *common sense*. That is why they are taken for granted and not challenged. But the fact that a practice has been there for a long time does not give it a license that it is appropriate as well. Being members of a dominant group, whatever men do or say is presented as standard and normal and, if women do it differently, their actions are dubbed as abnormal and deviant.

ROLES AND EXPECTATIONS

Following the same approach of binary division, women and men have been divided into two groups and certain attributes have been attached to them. According to Eckert and McConnell-Ginet (2003: 37):

> The opposition *larger-smaller*, for example, does not only differentiate male from female, but it operates within the male and female categories as well. Men who are small with respect to other men are viewed as less masculine; women who are large with respect to other women are viewed as less feminine.

Society thus views these two groups in a discriminatory manner and determines certain roles for them based on the societal view of their sex. Defining human beings through binary categories is challenged by Bing and Bergvall (1996: 1), who are of the opinion that, '. . . much of our experience does not fit neatly into binary categories, and is better described as a continuum with indistinct boundaries.'

A very common divide is the private/public role, where women are given the responsibility of the home and men are vested with the responsibility to earn bread for the family. Since the economic aspect is linked with men's responsibility, the centre of power is also shifted to them, which has significant implications for the rest of the social domains.

THE OPPORTUNITIES

The roles determined by society for men and women lead to certain expectations. Interestingly, these expectations are manufactured by society 'suitable' to the prestructured roles. For instance, a few years back, women in South Asia were not expected to fly fighter planes. It took a long time for women to be given the opportunity to work as fighter pilots. Since society has differing expectations from boys and girls, the opportunities given to them are based on these expectations which act as constraints to think beyond limited and stereotyped opportunities.

DISCOURSE AND GENDERED STEREOTYPES

These stereotypes about the gendered notions of society are constructed and perpetuated in various forms of discourses. Wodak (1997: 6) comments on the role of discourse in the construction of these stereotypes:

> Discourse is socially constituted, as well as socially conditioned—it constitutes situations, objects of knowledge, and the social identities of and relationships between people and groups of people. It is constitutive both in the sense that it helps sustain and reproduce the social status quo, and in the sense that it contributes to transforming it.

GENDER AS PERFORMANCE

Such discourse helps in performance of gender (Austin, 1962; Butler, 1990), which is not a fixed notion. Eckert and McConnell-Ginet (2003: 17) suggest that:

> Being a *girl* or being a *boy* is not a stable state but an ongoing accomplishment, something that is actively *done* both by the individual so categorized and by those who interact with it in the various communities to which it belongs.

This explanation alludes to a very important aspect of gender, that it is not just a thought which is abstract but it is actually *performed* by all of us consciously or unconsciously. According to Goddard and Patterson (2000: 4), '. . . people often put the blame for stereotyping elsewhere—for example it's in the language itself, it's the fault of the media, it's to do with the "society". They tend not to include themselves in their account.'

THE ROLE OF MEDIA

In contemporary technologically advanced communication systems, the process of stereotyping has gained tremendous speed and impact. The media, through its news, plays, commercials, discussion programmes, movies, and songs, is reinforcing the stereotypes by legitimizing them and amplifying their impact. The impact is so overwhelming that even the marginalized groups internalize the notions constructed against them by the dominant groups. This, according to Chomsky, is done through 'manufacturing consent'. Women are led to believe in a certain image of themselves, which has been created by agencies working for the dominant groups.

POLITICS OF DISCOURSE

Discourse, which is a central point in the theories of Foucault (1972, 1978, 1980) and Norman Fairclough (2001), is mainly constituted by language. In this way, language becomes a highly political phenomenon, which is linked with power. In the past, sociolinguists did not pay much attention to the role of language in construction of gender.

It is important to explore how language wields its power in constituting stereotypes. In every society there are certain stereotypes, which guide the masses along certain thought patterns. Stereotypes, in simple terms, are popular statements in a society which may not be true. Their strength lies in large-scale acceptability and frequent use by people. Stereotypes thrive on the major social institutions, including family, educational institutions, and religious institutions. In contemporary times, media has become a major agent in the process of socialization.

Media plays an important role in constructing gender ideology. According to Renzetti and Curran (2002: 162):

> . . . language and the media socialize us, and with respect to gender, much of this socialization takes place through *symbolic annihilation:* symbolically ignoring, trivializing, or demeaning a particular group, which in this case has traditionally been women.

According to Jackson, quoted in Hussein (2004: 103):

> . . . one feature of a gender ideology is that 'men and women' are relational, socially constructed, culturally septic and negotiated categories.

A more comprehensive definition is given by Hussein (2005: 59), who considers gender ideology as 'a systematic set of cultural beliefs through which a society constructs and wields its gender relations and practices. Gender ideology contains legends, narratives, and myths about what it means to be a man or a woman and suggests how each should behave in the society.'

POLITICS OF LABELLING

The politics of labelling confines the roles, and opportunities, for males and females. For instance, at a very initial stage, children are made to believe that games for boys and girls are different. The expectations of parents from their sons and their daughters, in terms of choice of professions, are different. Similarly, the ways males and females should speak are different.

The theorizing of gender has its own advantage as Wodak (1997: 35) maintains that:

> Theorizing gender and its relationship to language does not, in itself, dismantle the unequal and unjust social relations which are thereby revealed; one might hope, however, that in revealing them it contributes to the project of demystifying them, denaturalizing them, and so making it less difficult for feminists to change them.

THE EXAGGERATED DIFFERENCES

A large number of studies have focused on how women and men speak and the observation that they speak in different ways. The projected difference between males and females is reflected in the title of Gray's book, *Men are from Mars, Women are from Venus*, which became an instant best seller. There seems to be no harm in being different but the problem is that the touch stone, or standard is considered to be the language spoken by men. Thus, the language spoken by women is considered, not just different, but deviant and deficient.

DISCRIMINATORY LINGUISTIC TREATMENT

Table 4.3, referring to the traits assigned to males and females, is taken from Millet (1969: 230):

Table 4.3: Traits Assignable to Male (Instrumental) or Female (Expressive) Roles

	Trait	Pertains primarily to Instrumental (I) or Expressive (E) role	Trait is congruent (+) or incongruent (−) characteristic of role
1	Tenacity	I	+
2	Aggressiveness	I	+
3	Curiosity	I	+
4	Ambition	I	+
5	Planfulness	I	+
6	Dawdling and procrastinating	I	−
7	Responsibleness	I	+
8	Originality	I	+
9	Competitiveness	I	+
10	Wavering in decision	I	−
11	Self-confidence	I	+
12	Anger	E	−
13	Quarrelsomeness	E	−
14	Revengefulness	E	−
15	Teasing	E	−
16	Extrapunitiveness	E	−
17	Insistence on rights	E	−
18	Exhibitionism	E	−
19	Uncooperativeness with group	E	−
20	Affectionateness	E	+
21	Obedience	E	+
22	Upset by defeat	E	−
23	Responds to sympathy and approval from adults	E	+
24	Jealousy	E	−
25	Speedy recovery from emotional disturbance	E	+
26	Cheerfulness	E	+
27	Kindness	E	+
28	Friendliness to adults	E	+
29	Friendliness to children	E	+
30	Negativism	E	−
31	Tattling	E	−

LANGUAGE USED *ABOUT* WOMEN

A number of studies and books focus on the language used *by* women but the more important aspect which needs to be discussed is the language used *about* women. Studying the language used *about* women tells us a lot about the patriarchal set up of a society. It is important to note that gender is created on a day-to-day basis as we use language to carry out functions. Spender (1990: 106) suggests:

> The group which has the power to ordain the structure of language, thought, and reality has the potential to create a world in which they are the central figures, while those who are not of their group are peripheral and therefore may be exploited.

TITLES USED FOR MEN AND WOMEN

Natural and taken-for-granted expressions can be politically loaded. For instance, the titles used for a woman 'Miss' or 'Mrs', clearly reveal her marital status, whereas there is just one title 'Mr' used for a man, which in no way refers to his marital status. These apparently innocently assigned titles are in fact highly biased against women, as just a woman's title reveals the information she may not be ready to reveal voluntarily at the very outset. The two extracts are taken from a very popular Urdu book *Bahishti Zevar* by Maulana Ashraf Ali Thanvi. The book was essentially written for Muslim women. In the given excerpts, certain salutations are proposed for writing letters to husbands and wives. It is interesting to note that, in writing a letter to a husband, one of the recommended salutation is 'Long live my lord', whereas a husband writing a letter to his wife may use the salutation 'the embellishment of my home'. These salutations refer to the contrasting statuses and roles of women and men.

﷽ شوہر کے القاب و آداب ﷽

سردارِ من سلامت۔ السلام علیکم ورحمتہ اللہ بعد سلام اور شوق کے عرض ہے کہ محرمِ اسرار انیس غمگسارِ من سلامت۔ السلام علیکم ورحمتہ اللہ۔ بعد سلام نیاز کے التماس ہے۔ واقفِ راز ہمدم و ہمبازِ من سلامت۔ السلام علیکم ورحمتہ اللہ۔ اشتیاقِ ملاقات کے بعد عرض ہے۔

Translation

SALUTATIONS AND GREETINGS FOR HUSBAND

- Long live my lord. Peace and blessings be upon you.
- After greetings and love it is stated. . .
- Long live the custodian of my secrets and my compassionate friend
- Peace be upon you. After greetings it is requested. . .
- After my humble greetings it is stated. . .
- Long live my partner, knower of my secrets . . . Peace be on you.
- Desirous of seeing you, I state. . .
- Peace and blessings be upon you.

Thanvi, *Bahishti Zevar* (Heavenly Ornaments), 1997, Part 1, p. 18.

﷽ بیوی کے القاب و آداب ﷽

محرمِ راز ہمدم و ہمبازِ من سلامت۔ السلام علیکم ورحمتہ اللہ۔ بعد اشتیاق وتمنائی ملاقات کے واضح ہو کہ رونقِ خانہ و زیب کا شانہء من سلامت۔ السلام علیکم ورحمتہ اللہ۔ بعد شوقِ ملاقات کے واضح ہو۔ انیسِ خاطرِ غمگین تسکین بخش دل اند وہگین سلامت۔ السلام علیکم ورحمتہ اللہ۔ بعد اشتیاقِ ملاقات کے واضح ہو۔

Translation

SALUTATIONS AND GREETINGS FOR WIFE

Long live my partner, knower of my secrets.

- Peace and blessings be upon you . . .
- Curious and desirous to meet you . . . be it clear to you . . . Long live O' life and embellishment of my home
- Peace and blessings be upon you. After sharing my longing to meet you, be it clear to you.
- May you live long O friend of my gloomy heart, and solace of my melancholic soul.
- Peace and blessings be upon you. After sharing my longing to meet you, be it clear to you.

Thanvi, *Bahishti Zevar* (Heavenly Ornaments), 1997, Part 1, p. 19.

SET ROLES FOR WOMEN AND MEN

As discussed before, gender is made up by society through construction of roles, expectations, and opportunities for males and females in separate ways. When we come across terms like *doctor*, *warden*, etc., a male image comes to mind. That is why we use the expressions *lady doctor* or *lady warden* to ensure that we are talking about women. These linguistic expressions suggest how certain roles are attached with a certain gender.

INFLECTED EXPRESSIONS FOR WOMEN

It is interesting to note that most of the words used for women are derivatives of the expressions used for men, e.g., director/directress, actor/actress, poet/poetess, etc. This trend suggests that the central expressions were for men and expressions for women are inflections of those expressions. Goddard and Patterson (2000: 61) point out that:

> There are other forms of marking that are more clearly part of the **morphological** system of English: for example **suffixes** such as 'ess' and 'ette'. We have pairs of terms where the unmarked form is male, and the marked form female. Not only does this suggest that the male

figure is the 'norm' and the female one 'deviant', but the female form clearly has derived status and, in the case of 'ette', implies diminution or imitation. . . .

Goddard and Patterson (2000: 61) produce a list of pairs of terms to support the above point:

Table 4.4: Pairs of Terms for Males and Females

Manager	Manageress
Usher	Usherette
Actor	Actress
God	Goddess
Lad	Ladette
Waiter	Waitress
Mayor	Mayoress
Master	Mistress

MISTER TO MISTRESS

It is important to observe that an expression used for men sounds normal but when it is inflected to be used for women, it attains negative connotations, e.g., when the expression 'Mister' for men becomes 'Mistress' for women, it instantly becomes negative.

COLLOCATION

When female and male expressions are used, usually the male expression comes first, for example, 'men and women', 'he and she', etc. The constant use of this sequence may help in internalizing the order of superiority in an indirect manner.

NEGATIVE EXPRESSIONS FOR WOMEN

It is important to understand that words have their literal and connotative meanings. The connotation of a word refers to its associated meanings which are bestowed by society. Like gender, connotations are also socially constructed. For similar situations, there are different words for men and women, with different connotations. For instance, a man who is not married is called a *bachelor*, which is a respectable expression in a society. On the other hand, a woman who is not married is called a *spinster*, which has a negative connotation, suggesting that perhaps there was something lacking in the woman.

POSITIVE TO NEGATIVE CONNOTATIONS

In some cases, the same expressions, when used for men, bear positive connotation but, when used for women, carry a negative connotation. For example the expression *outgoing*, in subcontinental culture, has positive connotation when used for men and a negative connotation when used for women.

BIASED PROVERBIAL USE

In our sayings and proverbs, certain positive and socially desirable expressions are linked with men. For instance, 'be a man' is used to instruct someone to act bravely. But attributes of weakness are linked with women. For instance 'don't cry like a woman' would be a taunting remark for boys.

MASCULINE EXPRESSION AS NORM

Male expression has become so powerful that we take it for granted that women need not be separately mentioned. For instance, expressions like, 'man-made things' or 'mankind', etc., have no mention of women, as it is taken for granted that women are included. This apparently harmless linguistic gesture is one of the many devices used to exclude women and turn them into taken-for-granted entities. With a little effort, one can identify a number of such expressions.

GENERIC MASCULINE PRONOUN

Similarly, the generic masculine pronoun *he* is used indiscriminately, taking women for granted. One shocking example is the following paragraph about the eligibility of voters in Article 51(2) of the Constitution of the Islamic Republic of Pakistan. Throughout the text, the pronoun *he* is used and women are taken for granted

A person shall be entitled to vote if—
(a) he is a citizen of Pakistan;
(b) he is not less than eighteen years of age;
(c) his name appears on the electoral roll; and
(d) he is not declared by a competent Court to be of unsound mind.

Reading the above lines, the impression one gets is that it is only male members of the society who are eligible to vote. All these examples suggest that language is actively involved in construction and perpetuation of gender stereotypes.

Chapter 5
Growing Up With Gender

Young children experience that which comes to them, they adjust themselves to it in an immediate fashion, without there being present in their experience a self.

– George H. Mead

The potential consequences of the different childhood cultures produced by early sex-segregated play groups are significant not only for development in childhood, but considerably beyond, particularly when the two sexes converge in adolescence and adulthood.

– Fabes et al.

Gender is a social construct which is fluid and variable in relation to time and space. Like any other social learning, we acquire the notion of gender as a part of cultural knowledge. The major culture-constituent forces include the social institutions that construct, validate, and perpetuate social knowledge. The first social institution that the newborn are exposed to, is their family. It is the family which instils in the child's mind the essential attributes associated with male and female. Kane (2006: 149–150) claims that:

Parents begin gendering their children from their very first awareness of those children, whether in pregnancy or while awaiting adoption. Children themselves become active participants in this gendering process by the time they are conscious of the social relevance of gender, typically before the age of two.

CATEGORIZATION ON THE BASIS OF SEX

Categorization on the basis of sex starts at the time of birth, when girls and boys are labelled and distinguished with pink and blue colours. According to Fabes (2004: 262), 'Sex segregation begins around the age of 3 years and escalates over childhood. By the time children enter pre-school, young boys and girls show strong and consistent preferences for same-sex peers over other-sex peers.'

At a very early stage girls and boys are subjected to differential treatment in the family. Nanda and Jagatdeb (2008: 16) note that:

Discrimination against South Asian women begins at, or before, birth. In many countries, gender selective abortion and infanticide are common. Sex selection before birth and neglect after birth and during childhood results in men outnumbering women. Female foeticide and infanticide, neglect of health and gender-biased feeding practices combined with heavy work burdens are manifestations of son preference that is sustained by patriarchal structures which prevail across the region.

ECONOMIC REASONS FOR PREFERENCE

In South Asian countries, where a large number of inhabitants are leading lives below the poverty line, sons are generally preferred over daughters for economic reasons. Further, because of the unfortunate custom of mandatory dowry, girls, especially in families with fewer resources, are considered as a burden. Children, when they start growing, observe the environment and attitudes of their families. They keenly observe the relationship of their mothers with their fathers. They study the social roles very closely, e.g., who goes out to earn money? Who takes care of home? These early observations become an important source of social knowledge and children start internalizing the roles of males and females at a very young age. In families where domestic violence is common, children develop aggressive attitudes which, in some cases, remain with them for a long time. Besides observing the relationship of their parents, children acquire social norms from their siblings. A differential treatment in the family strengthens gender stereotypes in their minds.

THE PARENTAL ROLE

Parental attitudes can impact the process of gender development as the initial formation of self image takes place in the family. It is the parents who determine roles on the basis of sex, through their own example and through the treatment of their children. Tieger, quoted in Albert & Porter (1988: 187), suggests '. . . on the basis of a review of cross-cultural literature that parents differentially socialize males and females virtually from birth and that parental gender stereotypes cause the development of gender differences in aggression.'

Similarly it is the parents who associate a set of expectations with their sons and daughters. In South Asian countries, most of the parents would not like their daughters to talk loudly or laugh before strangers, whereas such conditions are not applicable to sons. Parents are also instrumental in providing different sets of opportunities to their children, e.g. in mainstream families in a South Asian country a son will face no problem in gaining parental permission for higher studies overseas, but parents are usually reluctant to send their daughters abroad for studies. Parental expectations regarding outlook, dress, job, responsibility, wedding, etc., generally differ on the basis of sex.

EARLY LESSONS IN GENDER ROLES

Early lessons of gender roles are taught in families when domestic chores are divided amongst the children on the basis of sex. The roles that are assigned and practiced in the family are internalized by girls and boys at an early age. These initial self-images remain with them even when they grow up. As a result of early internalization, a number of women would hesitate to bring a change in their lives by challenging the hegemony of male members of society.

In recent times, the popular Disney movies have their related characters available in the form of toys on the market. Lee (2008: 12), referring to a research study, claimed that the children '. . . learn much about themselves, other people, and society at large not only from their experiences in schools, but also through popular culture.'

Children establish emotional associations with these characters and they become a part of their real lives. Wohlwend (2009: 58), referring to the toy-reality relationship suggests that, 'One can be Cinderella all day long, sleeping in pink princess sheets, eating from lavender Tupperware with Cinderella decals, and dressing head to toe in licensed apparel, from plastic jewel-encrusted tiara to fuzzy slipper-sock.'

A symbolic divide on the basis of sex is apparent in the choice of games and toys. Toys are not just a source of entertainment but an effective education source. Singer (1994: 6) suggests that '. . . children's play, with its repetitive and exploratory characteristics, represents not only fun but a critically important feature of their development of cognitive and emotional skills.'

According to Martin et al., (1995: 1453) 'A consistent finding in the developmental literature is that children prefer toys traditionally stereotyped for their own sex more than toys stereotyped for other sex.' Toys and games for boys foster attributes like aggression, violence, and control, whereas those for girls cultivate the characteristics of organization, caring, sharing, cooking, baking, etc. In a study, Wegener-Spohring (1994: 90) observed that, 'Of the 218 boys interviewed, 165 (76%) owned war toys and 98 (45%) wanted more of them. Of the 211 girls interviewed, 61 (29%) owned war toys and only 7 (3%) wanted more.' In another study, Pellegrini and Jones (1994) concluded that the girls were significantly more likely than boys to engage in fantasy and use fantasy-oriented language. Actually, girls also engaged in fantasy more frequently than boys with both the male-preferred and neutral toys.

According to Carlson and Taylor (2005: 93):

> Around the world there are fairly consistent differences in the proportion of rough-and-tumble activity, aggression, and use of large spaces, all higher in boys, as well as cooperation, dyadic versus group play, and preference for fine motor toys, all higher in girls.

GENDERING OF THE BODY

Games and toys are closely related with gendering of body. Martin (1998: 495) observes that gendering of the child's body is '. . . the foundation on which further gendering of the body occurs throughout the life course. The gendering of the children's bodies makes gender differences feel and appear natural, which allows for such bodily differences to emerge throughout the life course.'

The choice of these games is approved by the parents. If girls try to move to boys' toys, they are discouraged, and vice versa. Boys usually play games in which they emerge as warriors, saviours, and heroes. Their games include guns, fighter planes, car racing, etc. On the other hand, girls prefer to play as teachers or cooks or bakers in the toy kitchen, or to apply make-up and comb their dolls' hair. Albert et al. (1988: 185) suggest that, '. . . young children make gender-typed classification of objects like toys, clothes, and household items at an even earlier age than they make gender-typed attributions of personal and social characteristics.'

SOCIAL CATEGORIZATION

Thus, the divide on the basis of sex is strengthened through social categorization. This social categorization leads to segregated social norms in living styles, e.g., an unorganized boy is acceptable as a norm in society but a girl has to be organized and tidy otherwise she is dubbed as ill-mannered and socially unacceptable. Katz (1985: 29) comments on this segregation and its repercussions:

> . . . the practice of labelling certain type of toys for boys only and others for girls only may be quite deleterious. Since toys do teach a variety of skills, the question becomes why we teach them unevenly.

Boys and girls are encouraged to grow in separate environments with different roles and expectations. This initial division at the family level is further strengthened by the social institutions of schools and print and electronic media. Stoddart and Turiel (1985: 1241) refer to the research of Marantz and Mansfield, who found that the younger subjects showed greater preference for same-sex stereotyped occupations and more stereotyping of activities than did the older subjects.

'CULTURAL' DIFFERENCE

Tannen (1992) proposes that girls and boys grow up in different cultures. That is why there could be potential misunderstandings when they converse with one another. These potential misunderstandings are due to the 'cultural differences' with which they were brought up.

Keeping in view the significant role of the family, as a social institution, it is crucial that differential treatment of boys and girls should be discouraged at a very early stage. The girls should be given confidence and opportunities to express their potential. This early realization for the need of mutual respect and recognition plays an important part in peaceful coexistence.

Chapter 6
Language and Gender: Research Directions

Language must be investigated in all the variety of its functions.
— Roman Jakobson

. . . new approaches share a concern with the complexity of actually occurring interactions, and therefore favor ethnographic and discourse-based methodologies over the traditional linguistics methods of native-speaker intuitions and carefully controlled experimental research.
— Hall and Bucholtz

Research on language and gender is not very old. An important early book in this regard was Jesperson's, *Language: Its Nature, Development, and Origin*, published in 1922. It contained a separate chapter about the language of women titled, *The Woman*, which suggested that the language of women is a deviant from the norm. The norm in this case was the language spoken by men. This kind of research emerged from an inherent assumption that women are inferior.

To support this common notion of male superiority, medical evidence was quoted, suggesting that a woman's brain is smaller than a man's brain. Hence, women are less intelligent. Brizendine, (2006: 23) in her book, *The Female Brain*, however, suggests that, although the female brain is smaller in size than the male brain, 'Women and men, however, have the same number of brain cells.'

The real impetus to the research in the area of language and gender, however, was given by the feminists. That is why we see a number of seminal books written specially on the topic of language and gender which have left a far-reaching impact on the field.

THE DEFICIT MODEL

Robin Lakoff was devoted to language and gender research. Her book focused on women's language and the attributes that makes it 'weak'. Some of the characteristics of women's language highlighted by Lakoff are:

1. A large stock of words related to their specific interests, generally referred to as 'woman's work';
2. Use of 'empty' adjectives like divine, charming, cute . . .;
3. Tag questions;
4. The use of hedges, e.g., 'well', 'you know', 'kind of', and so forth;
5. Use of the intensive 'so':
6. Hyper correct grammar;
7. Super polite form;
8. Women don't tell jokes;
9. Women speak in italics.

WOMAN'S DILEMMA

According to Eckert and McConnell-Ginet (2003: 1), Lakoff's earlier article written along the same lines '. . . argued that women have a different way of speaking from men—a way of speaking that both reflects and produces a subordinate position in society.' Lakoff talked about the dilemma that, on the one hand, society expects a woman to act 'lady like' and, on the other, when women speak in a lady-like manner, their language is dubbed as weak. Lakoff's approach to women's language is popularly known as a *deficit* approach as it considers that women's language is deficient.

Bergvall (1999: 277), critiquing the model, suggests, 'The DEFICIT perspective on gender variation has its roots in medieval notions of the chain of being: God above man, above women, above the beasts. Women were seen as a diminished copy of the original Adam. Women's language was thus also an imperfect, deviant, or deficient gloss on men's.'

CRITIQUE OF LAKOFF'S BOOK

Lakoff's book was criticised for its non-scientific research methods, as it heavily relied on 'introspection and linguistic intuition'. Lakoff herself mentions in the introduction to her book (2004: 40), 'The data on which I am basing my claims have been gathered mainly by introspection: I have examined my own speech and that of my acquaintances, and have used my own intuitions in analyzing it.'

The book was also criticised for dichotomizing language groups on sex basis. Despite this criticism, which largely comes through hindsight, Lakoff's book remains a central reference in the research on language and gender. It is interesting to see that just after the publication of this book, a large number of short courses, articles, books for women offered to train them on assertiveness. It was ironical that the model or standard to which all the training was geared was the assertive style of men. Spender (1998: 8), commenting on Lakoff's book, writes:

> She takes male language as the norm and measures women against it, and one outcome of this procedure is to classify any difference on the part of women as 'deviation'. Given these practices, it is unlikely that Lakoff could have arrived at positive findings for women, for any differences revealed, where a product of language or of sex, would be predisposed to interpretation as yet more evidence of female deficiency.

THE DOMINANCE MODEL

Followed by Lakoff, Spender wrote an influential book, *Man Made Language*. The book, instead of talking about the deficiency of women, focused on the dominance of men. Analysing English language Spender (1998: 23) claims that:

> The semantic rule which has been responsible for the manifestation of sexism in the language can be simply stated: there are two fundamental categories, *male* and *minus male*. To be linked with male is to be linked to a range of meanings which are positive and good: to be linked to

minus male is to be linked to the *absence* of those qualities, that is, to be decidedly negative and usually sexually debased.

The book claimed that the language differences between men and women are in fact their social differences in real life. Men play a dominant role in society and this dominance can be seen in their language use as well. Spender claims that (1998: 12), 'The English language has been literally man made and that it is still primarily under male control. . . .' Sunderland (2006: 15) quotes Spender's claim, 'I would reiterate that it has been the dominant group— in this case, males—who have created the world, invented the categories, constructed sexism and its justification and developed a language trap which is in their interest.' The relationship of language use and power groups is also ascertained by Goddard and Patterson (2000: 100), who, commenting on Spender's work, suggest:

> Dale Spender's focus on our written archives of language, such as dictionaries and grammar books, revealed the extent to which language is a socially constructed system rather than some natural phenomenon, and therefore can be used by powerful groups to encode their own meanings.

Like Lakoff, Spender dealt with men and women as two distinct groups. This model (based on Spender's book) is called the *Dominance Model*.

THE DIFFERENCE MODEL

A third book that influenced the discussion on language and gender was Deborah Tannen's, *You Just Don't Understand: Women and Men in Conversation*. According to Tannen (1992), men and women are brought up in two different cultures, i.e. man-specific and woman-specific cultures. This two cultures model is called *difference* model. Tannen (1992: 215) observes that:

Women and men feel interrupted by each other because of the differences in what they are trying to accomplish with talk. Men who approach conversation as a contest are likely to expend effort, not to support the other's talk, but to lead the conversation in another direction, perhaps one in which they can take centre stage by telling a story or joke or by displaying knowledge. . . . Women's effusion of support can be irritating to men, who would rather meet with verbal sparring.

MEN ARE FROM MARS, WOMEN ARE FROM VENUS

Just after this book, Gray's (1993) book, *Men are from Mars, Women are from Venus,* which reemphasised this thesis, was published. According to Gray (1993: 59–60):

You see, the Martian and Venusian languages had the same words, but the way they were used gave different meanings. Their expressions were similar, but they had different connotations or emotional emphases. Misinterpreting each other was very easy. So, when communication problems emerged, they assumed it was just one of those expected misunderstandings and that with a little assistance they would surely understand each other. They experienced a trust and acceptance that we rarely experience today.

It is different from deficit and dominance models in the sense that it does not blame either men or women. Its similarity to these models lies in that it also dichotomizes men and women on the basis of sex. Tannen's book became an instant bestseller, as people could relate to their daily life communication experiences. Elaborating on Tannen's model, Renzetti and Curran (2002: 141–142) suggest:

. . . women and men have different communication styles and different communication goals. Just as people from different culture speak different dialects, women and men speak different *genderlects*. Women, maintains Tannen, speak and hear a language of intimacy and connection, whereas men speak and hear a language of status and independence.

DIFFERENCE MODEL AND VERBAL HYGIENE

The book came under a lot of criticism by some feminist critics as the difference model, according to them, is not sensitive to the socio-political realities where men wield power because of their dominant social roles. Some feminist writers are of the opinion that the book does not appreciate the sociopolitical context of language. Their viewpoint is inspired by the thesis of verbal hygiene put forth by Cameron (1996: 37)

> Verbal hygiene for women comes in two varieties which are strikingly contradictory: career advice, which aims to improve the linguistic effectiveness of professional women, and relationship advice, which deals with communication difficulties in male-female interaction, particularly in the context of heterosexual relationships.

According to Bergvall (1999: 278), 'Critics of this "difference" approach pointed out that such a separate-but-equal, assign-no-blame approach, though valorizing women's contributions, effectively downplayed a social reality in which difference was not equally valued or tolerated (Henley & Kramarae 1991, Troemel-Ploetz 1991, de Francisco 1991, Freed 1992, Uchida 1992).'

EXAGGERATING THE DIFFERENCE

Gray exaggerated the differences between men and women, as evident from the introduction to his book (1993: 5):

> *Men are from Mars, Women are from Venus*, is a manual for loving relationships in the 1990s. It reveals how men and women differ in all areas of their lives. Not only do men and women communicate differently but they think, feel, perceive, react, respond, love, need, and appreciate differently. They almost seem to be from different planets, speaking different languages and needing different nourishment.

One can appreciate that the differences are exaggerated to the extreme. This is understandable as the writer, after painting a bleak picture of unassailable differences, gives some recipes to overcome the problem.

CHANGING QUESTIONS OF RESEARCH

For a long time, the focus of research on language and gender was on the *difference* of language (grammar, lexicon, pronunciation, etc.), as spoken by men and by women. Gradually, a more important question was focused, i.e. language used *about* women. This question raised the issue of power and representation. We see some useful research in the discriminatory use of language, i.e. naming, titles, use of generic masculine pronoun, and collocation, etc. But to appreciate the deeper level of the problem, we need to understand the politics of discourse and the hegemonic role of language. The research by Sunderland and Wodak, who approached the issue using the theoretical position of Critical Discourse Analysis and tried to trace the dynamics of hegemonic representation with special emphasis on the construction of discourse, is useful.

THE FEMINIST CRITIQUE OF LANGUAGE

The feminist critique on questions of language and gender came in the form of Deborah Cameron's edited book, *Feminist Critique of Language: A Reader* (1990). This book is structured around three themes, viz., the theme of silence and exclusion from language, the theme of naming and representation, and the theme of behavioural differences in language. Deborah Cameron's critical introductions to these themes are insightful. Hall and Bucholtz (1995: 9) suggest three directions of feminist research on language and gender. According to them:

Three general analytical stances in the new feminist scholarship on language: the investigation of how cultural paradigm of gender relations are perpetuated through language; the study of women's innovative use of language to subvert this dominant belief system; and the examination of how women construct social identities and communities that are not determined in advance by gender ideologies.

CONTEMPORARY TRENDS

Language and gender research is being done from different perspectives and focal points. Sunderland and Litosseliti (2008: 1), referring to *The Handbook of Language*, observe, 'the contributors draw on ethnography, grammatical analyses, discourse-based analyses, "discourse-historical" critical discourse analysis, conversation analysis, linguistic anthropology, text analysis, discursive psychology and "pragmatic eclecticism".' This large variety of methodologies in research on the one hand shows growing interest in the field and at the same time suggests the complex nature of language and gender filed where research from different perspectives is required for a better and fuller understanding.

THE DYNAMIC APPROACH

The *deficit*, *dominance*, and *difference* approaches are followed by what Coates calls the *dynamic* approach. According to Coates (2004: 6), 'The fourth and the most recent approach is sometimes called the dynamic approach because there is an emphasis on dynamic aspects of interaction. Researchers who adopt this approach take a social constructionist perspective.'

The contemporary stance on language and gender is more interdisciplinary in nature as the question of power needs to be explored from various different angles. The other change is that instead of dividing men and women on the basis of sex into two distinct groups, the researchers realize the significance of subgroups not formed strictly on the basis of sex. A third change is that instead of focusing on the language used *by* women, the emphasis is shifted to language spoken about women, i.e. the question of representation has come to the forefront.

PART 3

LANGUAGE, GENDER, AND SOCIETY

Chapter 7
Literature and the Politics of Exclusion

The silence of women is above all an absence of female voices and concerns from high cultures. If we look at a society's most prestigious linguistics registers—religious ceremonial, political rhetoric, legal discourse, science, poetry—we find women's voices for the most part silent—or rather, silenced, for it is not just that women do not speak: often they are explicitly prevented from speaking, either by social taboos and restrictions or by the more genteel tyrannies of custom and practice.

– Deborah Cameron

The great change that has crept into women's writings is, it would seem, a change of attitude. The woman writer is no longer bitter. She is no longer angry. She is no longer pleading and protesting as she writes.

– Virginia Woolf

Human history is full of struggles between different interest groups. Marx views history as a constant class struggle with different classes engaging in different tactics to acquire, sustain, and resist power. A more recent interpretation is offered by Bourdieu, who considers that the constant human struggle is for *social distinction,* which finds its ways through culture and education. A number of ways and means are adopted to gain supremacy and dominance over others groups. One fundamental method is to exclude 'others'. The process of exclusion is constituted by the use of various social institutions, including educational institutions, law making/ interpreting organizations, interpretations of religion, and print and electronic media.

EXCLUSION IN REAL LIFE

Historically, the caste system was a powerful system of exclusion, where a certain caste was completely barred from 'respectable' chores of life. This lower class was the class of 'untouchables' and arrangements were made to keep them at a distance. This desire of excluding others is reflected in different forms. For instance, in most public offices in Pakistan, washrooms for *officers* and *staff* are different. One recent example in the politics of Pakistan was the exclusion of most of the national population by passing a law making a Bachelors degree mandatory for contesting elections for national and provincial assemblies. In 2008, a large number of interested candidates could not participate because of this condition. Later on, the condition was removed because of public pressure.

THE NOTION OF 'SILENCE'

Another concept linked with exclusion is 'silencing' when a certain group is pushed to an extent that they are deprived of the roles and opportunities to voice their feelings. The structures are designed, through language, education, and culture, in such a manner that the marginalized groups find it difficult to come up to the standards set by the dominant groups and thus are handicapped for participation in the social arena of politics and power. Commenting on the over emphasis on differences based on sex, Crawford (1995: 8) suggests that, 'The sex difference approach is an *essentialist* approach. That is, it views gender as a fundamental, essential part of the individual. Essentialism conceptualizes gender as a set of properties residing in one's personality, self concept, or traits.'

SILENCING OF WOMEN

Bing and Bergvall (1996: 16) claim that, 'Gender polarization makes it easier to limit opportunities and exclude girls and women from education, public office and the military and easier to deny them legal protection and highly paid positions.'

A pertinent example is the silencing of women in the domain of writing literature in the past. Women were not encouraged to write literature as writing literature was considered not worthy of ladies. Woolf, in her essay, *Women and Fiction*, that first appeared in 1929 and was reproduced by Cameron (1990: 34), talks about certain periods of silence in the history of women writing. She focuses on sixteenth-century England when 'the dramatists and poets were most active, the women were dumb.

Cameron explores the reasons for the long silent periods when no female writings were available. According to Cameron (1990: 4):

> The silence of women is above all an absence of female voices and concerns from high culture. If we look at a society's most prestigious linguistic registers—religious ceremonial, political rhetoric, legal discourse, science, poetry—we find women's voices for the most part silent—or rather, *silenced*, for it is not just that women do not speak: often they are explicitly *prevented* from speaking, either by social taboos and restrictions or by the more genteel tyrannies of custom and practice.

POWER AND RULES

In asymmetrical relations between groups, the rules are always set by the more powerful. These rules are often biased against the marginalized groups and are bound to favour the interests of the dominant ones. The dominant groups in a society do not necessarily represent the majority but it is power that gives them the 'right' to set the rules of the game. It is to the advantage of the dominant groups to share the fruits of power in a smaller group by excluding 'others', These mutual differences are highlighted, and at times created, to exclude others through making categories and labels and setting up norms, and standards that favour the dominant groups.

LANGUAGE AND EXCLUSION

According to Woolf (1990: 34), 'law and custom were of course largely responsible for these strange intermissions of silence and speech'. Other potential factors could be education and language, which play vital parts in constructing, legitimizing, and perpetuating certain stereotypes. These categories are constructed in such a manner that one category appears superior and the other looks inferior, e.g., good and bad, superior and inferior, etc. The architects of these categories are usually the dominant groups of society, who possess the discourse and the 'legitimate knowledge'. This legitimacy of knowledge is certified by the socially accepted educational institutions in a society. The hegemony coming from educational institutions, through a certain brand of education, is so powerful that Bourdieu had to identify it with 'symbolic violence'.

DISCRIMINATION THROUGH LANGUAGE

The class differences, the boundaries, and the categories are constructed, magnified, and perpetuated by the educational system in an effective manner. This is done through favouring dominant culture, language, curriculum, and pedagogical practices. Ultimately, the marginalised groups with meagre resources, are excluded as they are deprived of the opportunities of getting into such educational institutions. Most of the governmental steps are based on rhetoric and are shallow in their impact as Uks report (2002: np) notes that:

> Women friendly policies are occasionally introduced, but while well intentioned, they tend to be superficial and do not go beyond the surface. Those responsible for implementing them are forced to compromise. . . . up against a wall of political expediency and social prejudice reinforced by the media. However, any efforts to bring women's issues centre-stage, and to increase their visibility, contribute to a greater feeling of freedom in the society.

UTILIZATION OF FEMALE POTENTIAL

The history of Urdu literature in the Indo-Pak subcontinent is not very old. Although we find mention of poetry and prose even in the fourteenth century, the formal books in different genres of Urdu literature started appearing in the eighteenth century. The initial phase of Urdu literature is generally silent in terms of female voices. There are, however, some exceptions in two strands of female community during this period. The first strand comprised queens and princesses, belonging to different royal dynasties, who would compose poetry. The other strand consisted of courtesans, who exhibited great taste for literature and some of them actually wrote poetry. In both of these strands the impact of the social pressures of society was diluted for different reasons.

THE PHASE OF SILENCE

Female silence in mainstream literature owes to a number of silencing factors. Women in the Indo-Pak subcontinent were not given access to formal education. The only kind of education girls were permitted was religious instruction which, in most cases, was quite rudimentary, i.e. only recitation of the Holy Book. Women were confined to their homes and going to schools and working in offices was simply unthinkable. In this highly patriarchal system, literature was not considered suitable for women and writing literature was taboo.

WOMEN WRITING WITH PSEUDONYMS

The social pressure of mainstream society was such that some women had to write with male pseudonym. For instance Akbari Begum's first story *Guldasta-e Muhabbat* (Bouquet of Love) was published in 1903 under the pseudonym of Abbas Murtaza. Another story of the same writer, *Godar ka Laal* (Gem of the tattered clothes) was published under the name 'Mother of Afzal

Ali' (Jameel, 2002: 52). A similar anecdote is narrated by Hameed (2007: 380) about a novel *Islah-un-Nisa* (Reformation of Women), written in 1881 by Rasheeda-tun-Nisa, which could not be published on time because of the non-acceptability of a woman as novelist. Finally, it was decided to write the name of a male relative of Rasheeda as author. Years after publication, it was discovered that the novel was actually written by a woman. Hameed (2007–8: 15) describes the status of women in United India by suggesting that a woman was, '. . . educated only in matters of household concerns and meant only to know "just enough", her talent was either wasted, redirected towards something "more suitable" to her gender, or safely tucked away under the garb of a fictitious name.' This situation prompted men to undertake the job of representing women. Interestingly some male writers used *rekhti*, a kind of poetry that has a female narrator, employs the feminine language and claims to express the feelings and sentiments of women.

REPRESENTATION OF WOMEN

Said (1978: xii) quotes Marx as saying, 'They cannot represent themselves; they must be represented'. It is interesting to note that some male authors started the job of representation by prescribing and telling women how to speak, act, and behave. Nazeer Ahmed's novel *Mirat-ul-Uroos* (Mirror of the Bride), published in 1869, was specifically written for girls/women to encourage 'correct' and socially acceptable behaviour. It is a story of two sisters, Akbari and Asghari. Akbari is the elder sister, who is dubbed as unwanted, as she follows her moods. On the other hand, Asghari, the younger sister, living in a joint family system, always tries to please others and in the process sacrifices her personal pleasure. This novel thus reflects the attributes of a good girl or a good woman.

BAHISHTI ZEVAR (HEAVENLY ORNAMENTS)

Written on similar didactic lines, but a more popular non-fiction work, was *Bahishti Zevar* (Heavenly Ornaments) by Maulana Ashraf Ali Thanvi. Maulana Thanvi was a famous religious scholar, who wrote this book specifically for married Muslim women. The book, becoming very popular, was an integral part of the dowry that parents in Muslim families would give their daughters on the occasion of their marriage. Thanvi (1997: 54) gives a list of dos and dont's for girls and women in all walks. Some forbidden readings include:

- books of *ghazals*
- *Indar Sabha* (first Urdu play)
- *Dastan-e-Ameer Hamza*
- *Qissa Badar Muneer*
- novels
- newspapers

Women are also discouraged from reading novels and newspapers as a waste of time. One of the major reasons for forbidding such literature for women was that such books of poetry and fiction dealt with love stories and relationships between males and females.

DEFYING THE RESTRICTIONS

The first significant female voice in Urdu literature was that of Rasheed Jehan (1905–1952), two of whose stories were published in a book of short stories entitled *Angare* (Burning Coals). This book, which contained ten short stories on provocative social themes, was published in Lucknow in December 1932. It created instant ripples in literary and social circles and invited unprecedented protest by religious spokespersons. The book contained a story *Dilli ki Sair* (A Tour of Delhi) and a play *Parde ke Peeche* (Behind the Veil), by Rasheed Jehan. Both the writings addressed some basic but taboo issues of women's suppression and consequent female revolt. The book was banned on 15 March 1933, just three months after its publication. According to Mahmud (1978: 15), 'After the government's decision, police burnt all copies of the book except five copies, of which three copies were kept in the record room of Delhi and two were sent to London.' Rasheed Jehan, whose bold arrival in mainstream Urdu literature shocked many, was a qualified doctor, which was a rare phenomenon in the India of 1930s. Commenting on Rasheed Jehan's contribution in *Angare*, Jameel (2002: 57) writes:

> Women were restless even before the publication of 'Angare' but they did not have the courage to reverse the tide of circumstances. A favourite theme of Rasheed Jehan's short stories was the helplessness of middle class women and she portrayed this theme with confidence. This was made possible because of her intimate observation as a member of progressive writers' movement. Rasheed Jehan criticized the actual causes of women's backwardness, helplessness, ignorance, and defeated outlook.

SHORT STORIES

Ismat Chughtai (1915–1991), another female voice raised against the imposed restrictions, belonged to an unorthodox family where there was space for girls to express themselves without much inhibition. Ismat Chughtai wrote short stories and novels. She tried to challenge some of the stereotypes and dealt with forbidden themes. Her short story *Lihaf* (Quilt), published in 1941, was banned on the pretext of obscenity, because she touched on the theme of lesbianism. Her bold treatment of social issues in fiction was considered as 'un-ladylike' and most school libraries were reluctant to keep her books. Similarly, it was not considered appropriate for young girls to read her books. Later on, we see a number of female writers who enriched the genre of the short story in Urdu literature. Some of these names include Hijab Imtiaz Ali,

Mumtaz Shireen, Hajra Masroor, Khadija Mastoor, Jamila Hashmi, Bano Qudsia, Altaf Fatima, Khalida Hussain, Razia Fasih Ahmed, Zahida Hina, and Nilofer Iqbal.

FEMALE NOVELISTS

We find that some of the greatest novels in Urdu were produced by female writers, for instance, *Aag ka Darya* (Qurratulain Hyder), *Terhi Lakeer* (Ismat Chughtai), *Raja Gidh* (Bano Qudsia), *Aabla pa* (Razia Fasih Ahmed), *Dasht-e-Soos* (Jamila Hashmi), and *Dastak na do* (Altaf Fatima), etc. *Aag ka darya* (River of Fire) is considered one of the finest novels produced in Urdu. The novel, in terms of its scope, themes, diction, and treatment, has been attracting readers and critics alike since its publication in 1959. Qurratulain Hyder did not feel comfortable living in Pakistan and decided to migrate to India.

The tradition of female writers engaged in writing some great novels in Urdu literature resembles the English literature tradition, where female writers wrote some memorable novels. Woolf (1990: 35) gives an interesting justification for this:

> Fiction was, as fiction still is, the easiest thing for a woman to write. Nor is it difficult to find the reason. A novel is the least concentrated form of art. A novel can be taken up or put down more easily than a play or a poem. George Eliot left her work to nurse her father. Charlotte Bronte put down her pen to pick the eyes out of the potatoes.

WOMEN AND POETRY

As with English literature, we do not find prominent female poets in the early phase of Urdu literature either. Perhaps, of the different forms of literature, poetry was considered as something socially undesirable for women to read and write. Traditional Urdu poetry, largely written by male poets, presented a stereotypical picture of women. Ahmad (1990: ii) draws that picture in these words:

> A feckless beloved who was endowed with heavenly beauty reigned: fair of face, doe-eyed, dark haired, tall, willowy, for whom the poet was willing to die but who vacillated from indifference, shyness, and modesty to wanton wilfulness and cruelty. It was stylized and charming-tradition but it was also hidebound in its strictures, formalism, and usage.

But, as time passed and pressures of society became diluted, we hear some important female voices, which have made rich contribution to Urdu poetry. Ada Jaffery came with an original feminine voice. Similarly, Kishwar Naheed wrote about hitherto taboo topics for women. But the book that created the most ripples was Fahmida Riaz's, *Badan Dareeda* (The Torn Body). This was a collection of poems frequently dealing with intimate themes in a creative diction.

Later on, Fahmida Riaz was obliged to go into self-exile for a long time. Writing about her poems that talk about the woman's body, Riaz (2003: 35) explains, 'The different organs of the female body are referred to in these poems not as 'objects' but as being part of a woman's body. Symbols are not used because in the poem these organs themselves become symbols of a passion and denial.'

THE GRASS IS REALLY LIKE ME*
Kishwar Naheed

The grass is also like me,
It has to unfurl underfoot to fulfil itself,
But what does it prove by getting soaked:
A scorching sense of shame,
Or the heat of emotion.
The grass is also like me,
As soon as it can raise its head,
The lawn owner,
Obsessed with flattering it into velvet,
Mows it down again.
How you strive and endeavour
To level woman down too!
But neither the earth's nor woman's
Desire to manifest life dies.
Take my advice: the idea of making a footpath was appropriate,
Those who cannot bear the scorching defeat of courage,
Are grafted onto the earth.
That's how make way for the mighty,
But they are merely straw,
Not the grass,
The grass is really like me.

To: Daughter, Sheely*
Sara Shagufta

Whenever someone gives you a sorrow
Name that sorrow, 'daughter',
When my grey hairs appear
Laughing around your cheeks, you can weep
On the sorrow of my dream, you can sleep
Those fields which are yet to grow
In those fields
I see your brassiere too.
I was afraid
But only the first time, daughter
How many are the times I felt afraid daughter
Trees hide the archers who lie in wait for you
You were my birth, daughter
And your birth, your daughter will be
In the desire to bathe you
My fingertips spit blood.

VIRGIN*
Fahmida Riaz

The sky glows white like heated iron
The sand is dry as a parched thirsty tongue
Thirsty is the throat, the body, life itself.

My head bowed, I sit in the scalding desert
I have brought under your command this sacrificial animal!

The sacrifice which was obligatory on me, I have made.
There is still a glow in his bulging eyes
Its black hair is still soaked with blood
You had ordained that it should be unmarked
So it was, faultless, untouched and unseen too.
The warm blood absorbs in the endless sand
Look, it has stamped a stain on my 'chadur'.

O Great God
O Imperious one
O Proud and Angry One
Yes, I read your names and slaughtered it
Now let a shred of cloud come, let there be shade somewhere
O Great God
A breath of solace! For the soul itself is on fire!
A drop of water, for life is ending toward its end.

*Translated from Urdu by Rukhsana Ahmad in *Beyond Belief: Contemporary Feminist Urdu Poetry*: (1990)

Parveen Shakir (1952–1994), another Urdu poet, became instantly popular with her very first collection of poetry, *Kushboo* (Fragrance). In her later collections, *Sad Berg*, *Inkar*, and *Khud Kalami* she emerged as a mature poet who would present social issues with the romantic softness of Urdu *ghazal* and *nazm*. Parveen, an icon of female verse during her lifetime, spent an unhappy conjugal life that ended with divorce. She died at the age of 42 in a road accident.

Sara Shagufta was another female poet who wrote unorthodox prose poems in an innovative style. She experimented with the themes, diction, and form of her poetry. Her collection of poems, *Ankhein* (Eyes) is a reflection of creative genius. As we look at the Urdu poetry scene, we come across some important names who contributed to enrich Urdu poetry with the selection of new themes and diction. Some of these names include Ada Jaffery, Zehra Nigah, Kishwar Naheed, Fahmida Riaz, Parveen Fana Syed, Parveen Shakir, Shabnam Shakeel, Irfana Aziz, Nasreen Anjum Bhatti, Azra Abbas, Shahida Hasan, Fatema Hasan, Naheed Qasmi, Mansoora Ahmed, Shaheen Mufti, Samina Raja, and Yasmeen Hameed. These powerful voices brought new perspectives which have been hitherto absent in the Urdu literature.

POPULAR LITERATURE

Some female writers, however, focused on popular fiction. This kind of fiction is still very popular in magazines and digests especially written for women. Unlike the literature that challenged stereotypes, popular literature helped perpetuate gender stereotypes. This kind of fiction, that reflects the existing stereotypes, finds no opposition from society. Ahmad (1990: i) analyses the secret of the popularity of this kind of literature by women: 'In a society which is heavily male-dominated and devoted to the past, it is not surprising then, that the most popular female poets would be those who conform to both socio-cultural and literary traditions.'

PAUCITY OF FEMALE CRITICS

One important aspect of literature that needs more attention from women is literary criticism. It is important that women should be engaged in the process of writing literary criticism to appreciate and evaluate the texts written by male and female writers. We generally observe a paucity of female critics in Urdu literature. Ahmad (1990: i) rightly refers to

> . . . the conservatism of the literary establishment and their stranglehold on aesthetic values; their ability to dismiss work to which they cannot themselves relate and their inability to empathize with work that derives directly from women's experience.

If we look at the history of Urdu literature, we see only one female literary critic, Mumtaz Shireen, whose contribution in the field is valuable. A direct impact of having not many female critics also resulted in the exclusion of female writers from collections of literary works. Talking about this deliberate process of exclusion, Farooqi (2002: 17) concludes that, since the history of literature, like general history, has been dominated by men, the feminist perspective and literary works of women were consciously or unconsciously excluded from the list of literary works. These efforts to reclaim the silenced voice need to be strengthened.

Cixous (2000: 162) urged women to break the silence and express themselves by writing, 'And why don't you write? Write! Writing is for you, you are for you; your body is yours, take it.' Despite the strong silencing forces, female writers have come a long way and they now occupy a prominent position on the map of contemporary Urdu literature. Female engagement in the process of literary writing is important to ensure furthering of the cause of an unbiased discourse in literary circles based on the multiplicity of knowledge, experiences, and viewpoints.

Chapter 8
Sayings, Proverbs, and Women

. . . language is the primary means through which we maintain or contest old meanings, and construct or resist new ones.

– Eckert and McConnell-Ginet

Language is both material form and social practice: as the former, it is neutral shapes or syntagms; as the latter, it is constitutive of the discourses which are the mode through which social groups assert their values and express their experiences.

– Wykes and Gunter

South Asian countries have oracy-based societies, where people love to talk with one another. The role of spoken discourse becomes central in the process of communication. Conversation is considered an important component of the social fabric of these societies. People talk when they meet, travel, and interact, sometimes with certain objectives but most of the time just for the sake of it. In oracy-based societies the role of verbal narratives, anecdotes, sayings and proverbs becomes central in the formation of thinking patterns.

PROVERBS AND FOLK WISDOM

In literacy-based societies, written text acts as a primary source of reason and logic, whereas, in oracy-based societies, verbal tradition is strong and sayings, proverbs, and narratives are considered as important sources of reason and logic. They become a part of the folk wisdom, which acts as the authority of knowledge that gives legitimacy to certain notions, beliefs, and stereotypes. Fairclough (2001: 70) describes ideological common sense as '*common sense in the service of sustaining unequal relations of power*'. A proverb is defined by the Longman Dictionary (1978: 1102), as 'a well known phrase or sentence that gives advice or says something that is generally true'. The term *proverbial* is defined by the Longman Dictionary as 'well known and talked about by a lot of people.' According to Storm (1992: 168), 'Proverbs, it is said, are the fruit of a people's wisdom. Based on accumulated experience and transmitted from generation to generation, they reveal many hidden aspects of a people's culture and way of thought.'

POPULARITY OF PROVERBS

There are multiple reasons of the popularity of sayings and proverbs in a society, especially in an oracy-based society. They are short, simple, related to experience, use familiar vocabulary, clarify the idea, facilitate in communication, and above all legitimize the thought. According to Webster (1982: 173) 'Proverbs are the simplest of the metaphorical genres of folklore—song, folktale, myth, folk play, etc.—and the genre which clearly and directly is used to serve a social purpose.'

It is interesting to note that, on the one hand, proverbs gain legitimacy through their excessive use by the masses and, on the other hand, legitimize the communication of the people who use them. Proverbs facilitate the acquisition of social knowledge by making the otherwise difficult notions more palatable. Oha, cited in Hussein (2005: 61), quotes Finnegan's idea that, 'Proverbs are the palm-oil with which the words are eaten.' Proverbs are used as useful instruments to support the communication with the required logic and thus to enhance the impact.

The history of sayings and proverbs is ancient. Some very old proverbs are still active and effective in our society. The evidence of their ancient nature is the old lexicon used in the construction of these proverbs, which are otherwise not a part of our daily language. This suggests the powerful role proverbs can play to perpetuate some old stereotypes through different periods of time.

PROVERBS AND SOCIAL PRACTICES

If we look at a list of proverbs, we come to realize that a number of social practices are reflected in them. In this way, proverbs act as a mirror of what is happening in a certain society. Webster (1982: 175) is of the opinion that, 'Proverbs are part of the cognitive system of the culture in which they occur. They not only appear in a recognized form, but also contain references which are themselves cognitions.'

But they do not just reflect the outer action; rather, they are themselves involved in constructing a certain kind of social reality and in this way suggesting the ways of action to the different groups of society. Proverbs, in this role, become highly political as they pass judgements, attach expectations, and determine roles and limitations. All this is done with the authority of folk wisdom at their back. So, proverbs, on the one hand, act as the touchstone of truth and validate certain notions and, on the other hand, act as a monitor to pass judgement on people's actions.

GENDERED PROVERBS

Proverbs act as a tool to hegemonize the marginalized groups, especially women, in South Asian society. According to Hussein (2004: 129), 'Proverbs are used to ignore, trivialize and distort the image of women.' Let us examine some of the proverbs which represent women.

Proverb	Literal Meaning	Connotative Meaning
Jis mein chamak nahin who heera nahin, jis mein damak nahin who aurat nahi	A diamond without glitter is no diamond, a woman without a sparkle is no woman	The proverb refers to an unrealistic expectation of society from women, i.e. if a woman is not beautiful, she cannot be considered as a woman.
Aoont ki pakar aur aurat ke maker se Allah bachae	One cannot escape from a camel's grip and a woman's snare	The proverb on the one hand dehumanizes woman and on the other hand paints her as a treacherous character.
Beese Kheese, Satha Patha	A woman becomes weak at the age of twenty, whereas a man remains strong even at sixty	The proverb suggests the fast aging process of women because of malnutrition, extra stress, and physical labour.
Jaghre ki hein batein teen—zan, zar, aur zameen	Three things are likely to lead to quarrel: a woman, money, and land	The proverb brackets a woman with other property items like money and land.
Teesra beta raj rajae-teesri beti bheek mungwae	The third son helps you rule and the third daughter leads you to begging	The proverb suggests the unwelcome existence of a daughter as compared with a son. In the case of a son, more economic prospects are expected and there is no burden of dowry but, in the case of a daughter, (and that, too, a third daughter), there is extra economic pressure on South Asian parents in the form of dowry.
Taryamat mein jo nar aawe-who to apni lag gunwawe	A man who falls victim to a woman's advice loses his respect	It is important to observe in this proverb that man's social standing is measured by his disregard for the woman's counsel.
Yaar ko karoon piyar, khasum ko karon bhasum, lurkay ko karon chutni	Be in love with the lover, burn the husband and crush the son	This proverb is used for a woman with loose character. It talks about a woman who is not bothered about her husband and children and her only concern is her lover.

Proverb	Literal Meaning	Connotative Meaning
Aa parosun larein	Let us fight my neighbour	Woman is shown as a quarrelsome creature who likes to pick fights and if she can't find anyone within her house she invites her female neighbour to squabble.
Aaj kal bara bars ki bitya bar mangay	Nowadays even a twelve year old girl demands a husband/ with the changed times people have lost all decency	This proverb denotes the decadence of the modern times through the behaviour of women. The woman, conventionally associated with silence, becomes demanding, symbolizing loss of decorum in the new generation.
Aag lainay aiee ghar wali ban baithi	She came to borrow fire, became a consort instead/ took over the whole house on the pretext of borrowing something	Here a woman is represented as an intruder who pries into someone else's threshold and eventually becomes its domineering mistress. This proverb stereotypically brings out craftiness and guile as feminine characteristics.
Aankh mein thee sharam, dil ki thee naram	Shy and kind/A woman who modestly accepts even the most unreasonable demands	The conventional ideal image of a woman is modesty and gentleness. In short, she is represented as a person who effaces herself to suit the whim of others.
Aayee bee aaqila, sab kaamon mein dakhla	Entered the intelligent woman and the interference began/an ignorant prying woman	Pretence, ignorance and intrusion of women are being implied here.
Ugalti talwar aur baiswa lagai khasam ko maar rakhti hai	An unsheathed sword and an evil wife are an ever present threat to a man	The two domains of warfare and marital relationship have been brought together in this proverb. The bare sword is akin to an unrestrained female, hence symbolizing the paranoia associated with the emancipated woman.

Proverb	Literal Meaning	Connotative Meaning
Budhi ghori laal lagam	An old mare wearing a red bridle. An old woman donned as a young girl	Traditionally, youth is another societal construct through which a woman's acceptability is measured. The setting in of age thereby means a setting aside of interests that preoccupied her as a young woman otherwise she becomes an object of comment for the onlookers.
Bigra baita aur khota paisa bhi kabhi na kabhi kaam aa jata hai	Even a spoiled son and a false coin can work sometimes	The gender divide ascribes a significant place to a son in the family as compared to a daughter. Resultantly, this proverb regards even the most unworthy son as a blessing that would prove fruitful some day.
Bahoo rani kunwari, saas rahi wari, Bahoo aai biyahi par gai khawari	Before marriage the daughter-in-law is the apple of the mother-in-law's eyes, but after marriage begin the squabbles	In the Urdu/Hindi tradition, mother-in-law and daughter-in-law feuds are a subject of comment. This proverb alludes to this clichéd relationship and hence the quarrelsome and the unpredictable nature of women is being hinted at.
Biyahi baiti ka rakhna haathi ka bandhna hai	Keeping a married daughter at home is equivalent to tending an elephant/both result in increased expenses	The traditional logic presents daughter as an excruciating burden for the parents. Yet this proverb is interesting in terms of the economic question it raises in relation to gender.
Biyahi larki parosi dakhil	A married daughter is like a neighbour to her parents	This proverb brings to limelight a sense of non-belonging and displacement for married women. Women have to constantly define and redefine their sphere of existence. Here, the parents' house is portrayed as a foreign domain for a married woman in the aforementioned saying.

Proverb	Literal Meaning	Connotative Meaning
Aurat ki aqal gudi peechay	In the nape rest a woman's wits/A woman is dim-witted	Reason and intellect is another attribute generally related to men. This proverb builds on this reductive classification and relegates women to the other side of the scale as dim and senseless creatures.
Murghi ki bang kaun sunta hai	Whoever listens to a hen clucking?/ Whoever can rely on a woman's opinion?	This proverb displays an important societal bias against women. Unlike a cock who crows to declare his territory, a woman's judgement is deemed undependable. A woman as a result remains as a phantom voice in the background.
Jis ka dar wohi nahin ghar	A woman crosses all lines in the absences of the husband/ without the fear of her husband	This proverb defines the societal expectations and gender roles attributed to both husband and wife where the responsibility of a man appears to be that of domesticating his wife.

ESTABLISHING THE GENDER GAPS

These are just a few of a long list of sayings and proverbs that construct, legitimize, and perpetuate stereotypes on the basis of sex that determine the roles, expectations and opportunities for men and women separately. Bing and Bergvall (1996: 15) believe that, 'This oversimplification has traditionally been used to limit choices and opportunities for girls and women.'

Being part of folk wisdom, these sayings and proverbs establish and widen the gender gaps every time they are used. Being an important source of social knowledge, these stereotypes affect each segment of society, including women. The social knowledge perpetuated by the proverbs is also internalised by women. A large number of women start seeing themselves in the image constructed by the stereotypes contained by the gendered sayings and proverbs.

CHALLENGING THE STEREOTYPES

To challenge these stereotypes, we need to create awareness about the politics of this important source of social knowledge. We need to realize that proverbs are not necessarily based on ordinary life but represent the biases of dominant social groups. As proverbs, like all stereotypes, are strengthened with use, we need to be careful in using sexist proverbs. The other source of strength for proverbs is the legitimacy given to them by social institutions, e.g., family, educational institutions, media, etc. There is a need to challenge the gendered proverbs by all social institutions. It is through these means that we can alleviate the negative impact of such proverbs in our society.

Chapter 9
Gender and Jokes

> If we are to gain understanding, we must get out of these ruts; we must discard the vague notions of superiority, inferiority, equality which have hitherto corrupted every discussion of the subject and start afresh.
>
> – Simone de Beauvoir

> Ideology is most effective when its workings are least visible. If one becomes aware that a particular aspect of common sense is sustaining power inequalities at one's own expense, it ceases to be common sense, and may cease to have the capacity to sustain power inequalities, i.e. to function ideologically.
>
> – Norman Fairclough

The role of language as a highly political phenomenon in the construction and perpetuation of stereotypes, has been underlined in recent times by a number of scholars. Fairclough (2001), Pennycook (1994, 2001), Phillipson (1992) and others drew attention to sociopolitical aspects of language and its potential linkage with power and politics. The significance of *discourse* in the process of constructing a certain kind of social reality was brought forth by Foucault (1972) and was further strengthened by Edward Said in his phenomenal work, *Orientalism* (1978).

MAN-MADE LANGUAGE

The politics of representation, in which language plays a pivotal role, conveniently makes categories of good and bad, strong and weak, and normal and abnormal. Interestingly, like many tools of war, language is also possessed and used by the dominant groups of society, i.e. men. Dale Spender's book, *Man Made Language,* revolves around the thesis that male dominance in a society can also be seen in the domain of language use. Since language is made by men, they have the advantage of having the choice of positive words and phrases for themselves and a negative set of phrases and connotation for *others* (the marginalized groups), e.g., women.

JOKES AND STEREOTYPES

It is common knowledge that society impacts language but it is also important to understand how language impacts society by playing its role in constructing social reality by promoting certain stereotypes and perpetuating them. Stereotypes, in a subtle manner, make certain notions and beliefs a part of social wisdom and can be quoted as convincing arguments. These stereotypes are perpetuated in almost all forms of expression. One very powerful means of constructing and perpetuating stereotypes is humour and, more specifically, jokes. Jokes not only reflect the social norms, beliefs and trends of a society but they are also involved in constructing social realities and perpetuating them to the different spans of time. Jokes, being a popular form of humour, usually ridicule certain groups of society.

HEALTHFUL VS. HURTFUL HUMOUR

Like many stereotypes, jokes are usually targeted against the marginalized groups. Most such jokes lead to laughter at the cost of hurting the marginalized groups. Stereotypes, in the form of jokes, gain their strength through their repeated use by the masses and by the legitimizing effect of social institutions in general and media in particular. One such marginalized group that becomes the focus of jokes is women. A woman is turned into an object of laughter, as she is judged by the *standards* and *norms* set by men. Beauvoir

(1997: 16) disapproves of this approach and considers it unfair. She suggests that a woman is 'defined and differentiated with reference to a man and not he with reference to her; she is the incidental, the inessential as opposed to the essential. He is the Subject, he is the Absolute; she is the Other.'

INFLATED DIFFERENCES

The difference between women and men is magnified and highlighted through certain stereotypes. It has been claimed that male superiority is backed by superior anatomy. Brizendine (2006: 23), a practicing medical doctor, however, claims that, 'More than 99 per cent of male and female genetic coding is exactly the same.' This chapter analyses the politics of jokes about women. Before we look at some examples let us briefly examine the main effects of humour. Sultanoff (1995: Section 5) categorizes humour into healthful and hurtful humour. According to him:

> In general, healthful humour stimulates wit, mirth, or laughter. It creates closeness and intimacy. Hurtful humour creates pain and distance. Often healthful humour pokes fun at oneself and situations while harmful humour pokes fun at other individuals or groups. Sarcasm, put-downs, ethnic jokes, and anti jokes (anti-men, women, religious groups, nationalities, ethnicity, etc) are all considered hurtful, as opposed to therapeutic.

The majority of the jokes about women fall in the second category, i.e. harmful humour that leads to humiliation.

GENDERED STEREOTYPES

If we analyse jokes about women, we see certain underlying stereo-types at work. Some of the stereotypes about women include:

- Women are more talkative.
- Women are less intelligent.

- Women are capricious.
- Women are inquisitive.
- Women are cowardly.
- Women (as wives) are boring.
- Women are confused.

STEREOTYPES AND THE THOUGHT PROCESS

Though the above stereotypes do not have any scientific origin, they play a very vital role in the thought process of a society. The stereotypes categorize whole groups of women and men and assign attributes to groups rather than to individuals. Bing and Bergvall (1996: 16) point out that, 'The issue is not difference, but the denial of any differences within or across groups.' Goddard and Patterson (2000: 103) elaborate this point by suggesting that:

> . . . rather than a notion of femininity or 'masculinity', we should be thinking in the plural—of femininities and masculinities. This means that, rather than repeating the endless mantra 'women do this, men do that', we should be asking 'how does this group of men/women in this context enact their gender'?

JOKES AND GENDER STEREOTYPES

Jokes, in an apparently playful manner, perpetuate some serious stereotypes about women. The repeated use of these jokes turns the underlying stereotypes into folk wisdom. Let us look at the following jokes that make use of gendered stereotypes:

WIFE JOKES

Among women jokes, there is a subcategory of wife jokes. These jokes are based on stereotypical notions that a wife is a boring, dull, and troublesome creature. Let us see the underlying assumption (wives are troublesome) in the following joke:

Dr: Your husband needs complete rest. Take these sleeping pills.
Wife: When should I give these to him?
Dr: These are not for him but for you.

Let us look at another joke:

Wife: I wonder what will happen to you if I die.
Husband: And I wonder what will become of me if you don't die.

Yet another strain in jokes brings marriage and a graveyard together:

In a graveyard, a man sitting on his knees and holding on to a
tombstone was crying bitterly: 'Why did you pass away? Alas! I had
a bad fate that you died! Why did you leave, my God what should
I do? To where should I go? What could have gone amiss if you had
stayed on?'

A passerby on observing his agonizing outcry stopped by and said:
'Have patience. He appears to have been a very dear relative of yours.'

'No he wasn't. He was my wife's first husband', answered the first
man through his tears.

MARRIAGE AS A POINT OF RIDICULE

In jokes, marriage is treated as an institution deserving of ridicule.
Laughter is generated through a disruption of a supposed hierarchy.
The acceptable status of a man being superior as compared to his
wife is turned topsy-turvy and what is left is a man whimpering
for relief from a domineering wife. The first husband dead and the
other raising the dead are symbolic of a disrupted relationship and
the burden of responsibility is borne by the woman.

Wife: You love our dog more than you love me.
Husband: That's right. He does not bark as much.

A complaining wife is also an image that recurs in anecdotes to
provoke laughter. Here, a woman is represented as an insecure

and demanding creature, who needs even more assurance than an animal. Bringing an animal in comparison to the way a woman behaves is a replica of another derogatory comparison to which she is subjected.

> 'What does your wife say when you get back home late?'
> 'Nothing whatsoever.'
> How come?'
> 'I do not have a wife.'
> 'Then why the hell do you stay out till late at night?'

MARRIAGE AS A CONSTRAINT

Traditionally, where marriage is a way for women to be accepted into society, for men it is presented in the image of a confinement. Marriage for women is rendered as an elevation of status, while for men it is represented as an infringement on their freedom. A married man's late night venture is an escape from a curious and inquisitive wife while the same escape becomes a taboo for women.

> A man was shopping with his young daughter. His wife got left behind because of the crowd. When, after a thorough search, no signs of her appeared, the daughter began to worry about her mother.
>
> Weeping, she said to her father: 'Baba! We have left Ammi [Mother] somewhere behind. I am afraid she might get lost. She does not even know the way or the address of the house.'
>
> 'Don't worry!' the father said. 'If we find her, it's fine, otherwise I will get you a new one.'

A woman in this joke appears to be a dispensable object who can be substituted when lost. The significant aspect that needs to be discussed is the setting, i.e. a bazaar, where objects are sold and bought. The lost woman in a bazaar also stands for a social taboo that shows that, once having crossed the threshold, a woman's respectable position in society cannot be restored. Another persona is that of a daughter who questions what will become of the mother figure and the unconcerned reply, intended for amusement, is a reflection of the choice and decision that resides with a father figure.

WOMEN ARE TALKATIVE

A stone on the grave read: 'Here lies my wife. On 31st May 1982 her tongue was silent for the first time.'

The aforementioned grim humour exploits the most common stereotype about women, and especially wives, as talkative beings who do not give their husbands a chance to express their opinion.

If a lady happens to put the receiver down after only fifteen minutes, then what else can be inferred but that it was a wrong number?

Since jokes draw their humour from a repertoire of clichés, this joke is based on the stereotype of women as talkative figures. In this instance, gossip and useless chatter is a trope that comes to the feminine lot, and intends to generate amusement. The language of the statement presents this behaviour as a universal truth. Hence, it raises significant questions on the representation of the female figure. Humour in these statements depends on portraying women as indulging in useless activities and therefore it further weakens the position of women in society.

WOMEN ARE IRRATIONAL

A conversation was taking place between two women: 'This time we have seen the whole world. We will go somewhere else next time.'

The conversation of women in anecdotes is usually ridiculed for being snobbish and irrational. Here, a similar idea is endorsed where two women are projected through their unanimous conceit and absurd exaggeration in conversation. Their discontent also becomes a laughable matter, since it suggests that nothing on earth could satisfy their demands.

WOMEN AND TIME

> Husband: I am asking you for the last time, are you ready to come with me?
>
> Wife: I have been telling you for the past two hours that I'll be ready in a minute.

The punctual and awaiting husband depicts a committed man, who takes his work seriously, while the lazy and logically unsound woman coupled with him affirms a common misrepresentation of woman's indolent disregard for the value of time and commitment.

WOMEN ARE NOT INTELLIGENT

> A discussion was going on between girls and boys about lack of sense of humour in women. Girls were disagreeing with it. Suddenly, a boy stood up and announced in a decisive manner that girls lack a sense of humour. Explaining his view, he said that women laugh at every joke three times. First whenever someone cracks a joke. Second when the joke is explained and third when they understand it.

A common stereotype, popularized through different means of communication, is that women are slow or less clever and do not have a sense of humour. This stereotype has become the basis of a number of jokes.

> An alien came from another planet and inquired about the prices of different kinds of brains.
>
> Merchant: This is a monkey's brain, costs only 10 rupees.

Merchant: This is a man's brain, costs 100 rupees.

Merchant: This third one is of a woman.

Alien: How much does this cost?

Merchant: 500 rupees.

Alien: Why is it so expensive?

Merchant: It was hardly used.

The question of beauty and brains has always been associated with women. While, on the one hand, their beauty is projected as a criterion for acceptance in society, their brains remain as a butt of jokes. The aforementioned joke marginalizes woman by placing her intellectual capacity as inferior to that of both a man and an ape.

WOMEN AND AGE

During a case hearing in court, the judge questioned an accused woman about her age. The woman was reluctant to answer and was consequently warned by the judge: 'Take care; you are in a court of Law. You should clearly tell your real age while abiding by the oath of truth you have taken. What's your age?'

Woman: '32 years and a few months!'

Judge: 'What's "a few" months? Clearly specify the number of months!'

Woman: '60 months.'

Women and age are a constant topic of ridicule in jokes. Such jokes adhere to a stereotype that pertains to insecurity in women of growing old. In the aforementioned joke, a woman even when placed on a trial where truth might exonerate her, remains in denial of her true age. Interestingly, she is an accused woman, for whom owning to one's real age becomes equivalent to owning up to a felony. As a result, it can be assumed that what the woman is escaping from is exclusion in a society where youth is an inescapable expectation placed on her.

Here is another joke that is based on the stereotype that women are more conscious of their age.

> What is the way to silence a large crowd of noisy women?
>
> It's simple. Ask the question: 'Who is the eldest among you?'

MOTHER-IN-LAW JOKES

Jokes about mothers-in-law are not very common in South Asia as compared with the West. It appears that western literature draws more from this typecast. The reason may be attributed to the respect that is ascribed to woman as a mother in South Asian societies. Yet, the gradual perpetuation of this image cannot be denied, suggesting that the mother-in-law construct is an extortion of a prototypal westernized idea that gained roots with time in the Indo–Pak humour:

> One hunter shouted after his fellow hunter: 'Look! A lion is attacking your mother-in-law.'
>
> 'What an unlucky animal! She'll wreak havoc in his guts with her jabbering,' replied the second man.

The mother-in-law becomes a stereotypical woman figure in jokes, who is feared and detested by the son-in-law. She is rendered as an interfering and bossy presence in the household, who is always dissatisfied with her daughter's husband. The paradigm of the hunter and the hunted is extended in this joke to affirm the societal prejudice against women. The humour resides in constructing a woman as a hunter, rather than as a victim who is being preyed on. Interpreting the joke further, it alludes to another stereotypical role associated with mothers-in-law, i.e. match-making.

> Adam and Eve were the happiest couple of the world.
>
> Because they did not have a mother-in-law.

The mother-in-law is the oft repeated figure of an old woman projected as a precursor to quarrels and squabbles in family life. The very first man is therefore presumably the happiest, since there are no mothers to provoke family discord. Resultantly, woman is constructed as figure who aggravates friction in family relationships.

WOMAN AND STEREOTYPED WORK DOMAIN

'Did you get rid of your old dish washer?'

'Yes, I divorced her.'

The separation of domains, where a woman is supposed to deal with domestic chores while a man is the bread earner, is referred to in this joke. As a result, a woman becomes one of the many kitchen accoutrements that can conveniently be replaced when obsolete. The decision resides with the man, who is placed higher in the gender hierarchy by society.

WOMEN'S DESIRE FOR ADMIRATION

Women are constructed and presented in jokes in such a way as if their only interest and concern in life is adornment of their physical bodies in order to look good and get appreciation from others. This joke strengthens this stereotype in an apparently playful manner:

You tell any woman that she is looking beautiful and she will accept all other lies happily.

Let us look at another joke exploiting the same stereotype:

Once somebody asked the devil, 'You put people into different sorts of troubles. By this time, whom do you think you put in greatest troubles of all? The devil smiled and said, 'I gave one woman fifty pairs of shoes, fifty dresses, countless makeup items and got her married into a house where there were no mirrors.'

UNREALISTIC EXPECTATIONS FROM WOMEN

An expectation from women by the society is that every woman should be slim. Schultz (1990: 139) suggests:

> To be fat and sloppy is just as unforgivable in a woman as is being old, and the language has many terms designating such a person (are there any designating slovenly men?)—terms which have undergone pejoration and acquired sexual overtones at one time or another.

Let us read the following joke where this stereotypical expectation is active:

> A very fat lady was standing in the middle of the road. A car at some speed came and applied full brakes but still the lady was hit slightly and fell down on the road. The lady very angrily got up and started cursing the driver.
>
> Driver: 'I honked many times but you did not pay any attention.'
>
> Fat lady: 'You could have gone around me.'
>
> Driver: 'True, but I did not have that much petrol.'

Bruch, cited in Wykes and Gunter (2005: 7), alludes to a gendered stereotype expectation, that women should have a slim body, 'A thin body shape is associated with success personally, professionally and socially.'

WOMEN ARE CURIOUS

Another popular stereotype is that women are curious about others, especially about their friends or neighbours. The following joke is based on the stereotypical image of women:

> A postman knocked on the door. A beautiful woman came out.
>
> Postman: There is a parcel for Mrs Nasir Khan.

Lady: Is the parcel wrapped in expensive wrapper or in an ordinary paper?

Postman: In ordinary brown paper.

Lady: Who sent it?

Postman: Some Bushra Aziz.

Lady: From where?

Postman: Dadu, Sindh.

Lady: Any idea what could be inside?

Postman (irritated by this time): Why don't you receive it first and then see for yourself?

Lady: I can't, I am her neighbour, she lives next door.

STIGMATIZING 'OTHERS'

The dominant groups glorify their own stance and humiliate the *others* through jokes. Let us look at this joke that attempts to ridicule the female community:

Did you hear about the guy who finally figured out women?

He died laughing before he could tell it to anybody.

It is important to note that most of these jokes present women as boring and troublesome creatures and in an indirect manner describe men/husbands as innocent, helpless, and harmless beings. Cixous (2000: 164) points out the self-congratulatory tendency for men by suggesting that:

Nearly the entire history of writing is confounded with the history of reason, of which it is at once the effect, the support, and one of the privileged alibis. It has been one with the phallocentric tradition. It is indeed that same self-admiring, self-stimulating, self-congratulatory phallocentrism.

EXPECTATIONS AND REALITY

One of the sources of humour is incongruity. A number of jokes about women are based on the difference between *expectations* and *reality*. The dominant groups have a certain set of expectations for themselves and another set of expectations for *others*. Just like George Orwell's, *Animal Farm* (1987: 90), where 'all animals are equal but some are more equal than others', men in our society are *more equal*, as some really difficult attributes are expected from women. Some of the expectations from a woman in our society is that she should be beautiful, young, slim, and tall, with a fair complexion. These expectations are totally unrealistic and exert tremendous psychological pressure on women.

TECHNOLOGY AND ACCELERATED PERPETUATION

The process of perpetuation of gendered stereotypes has been accelerated in the modern technological era. In the past, the range of jokes was confined to a small number of people and stereotypes travelled at a slow pace. Now, with the advent of the Internet, one can access a number of sites dedicated to jokes. Besides the Internet, the ever-increasing number of mobile phones has accelerated the spread of jokes. The increase in circulation of jokes has made it possible for gendered stereotypes to reach a larger number of people in far less time.

NON-SEXIST JOKES

One may also come across jokes that target men. These jokes fall into another category, where marginalized groups give vent to their frustration through jokes. For instance, certain jokes become popular during the dictatorial rules. The jokes about men target their follies. Sexist jokes, whether they are against women or men, need to be discouraged. Students in schools and colleges should be exposed to the socio-cultural aspects of language as well. This awareness on the part of the learner and reader/listener may lead them to challenge and resist some of the gender-biased stereotypes created and propagated in the form of jokes.

Chapter 10
Matrimonial Ads: Societal Expectations

Taste classifies, and it classifies the classifier. Social subjects, classified by their classifications, distinguish themselves by the distinctions they make, between the beautiful and the ugly, the distinguished and the vulgar, in which their position in the objective classifications is expressed or betrayed.

– Pierre Bourdieu

People often put the blame for stereotyping elsewhere—for example it's in the language itself, it's the fault of the media, it's to do with 'society'. They tend not to include themselves in their account.

– Goddard & Patterson

Marriage has been a powerful institution in South Asia due to religious and socio-political influences. Historically, South Asian countries have enjoyed strong joint families and marriages were arranged by parents or elders. The girls' consent was not considered necessary if parents had decided about their weddings. Such marriages were possible, as girls were not exposed to education. Basu, cited in Khan (1999: 38), claims that 'As late as 1936, only 1.5% of the total female population in India was receiving some sort of education.' What little exposure to education there was, was confined to the urban areas and then mostly to primary education.

Besides lack of exposure to education, there was strong pressure from families, which were essentially patriarchal in character. Marriages would usually take place within families. The caste system was coercively compelling and marriage outside the caste was looked down upon in society. All these factors would come together to force a girl to 'agree' to an arranged match where in some cases the girl might not have even seen the boy before marriage.

EARLY MARRIAGES

The second tendency that dominated the marriage institution was early marriages, which could have potential negative effects on young girls. Sadik (2001: 18) comments:

> The imposition of marriage upon a young couple signals an effective end to their childhood or adolescence, and exposes a young wife to the grave risks associated with the physical dangers of early pregnancy and childbirth.

In South Asia, the tendency towards early marriages can still be seen in rural areas of the countries. The following data, quoted in the UNICEF Innocenti Digest (2001: 4), gives a glimpse of early marriage trends in some of the South Asian countries:

Table 10.1: Married Adolescents: Percentage of Married 15–19-Year-Olds

Country	Boys	Girls
Afghanistan	9	54
Bangladesh	5	51
Nepal	14	42
Source: UN Population Division, Department of Economic and Social Affairs, World Marriage Patterns 2000		

Early marriages would mean that the girl would have no proper education, the boy no proper job, and both of them would lack the requisite maturity needed for a smooth married life. Consequently, the elders of the family would direct and instruct the girl while the boy would be acting as a helpless observer.

All this was possible in the joint family system in vogue in most South Asia families. A girl, after marriage, was supposed to live in the large family of her husband, where she was to ensure that no one in the family should be displeased with her behaviour. This highly monitored environment, in the settling down phase of new life, would affect the marriage in a negative manner. The newly married couple would find few opportunities to spend time together and develop understanding on different issues

VOICELESS BRIDES

The third practice common in South Asian societies was the voicelessness of girls. Disagreement with husbands was not encouraged by society. The act of divorce was simply unthinkable and the life of a divorced woman could become miserable. Divorce would not only bring a bad name to the girl but would put a stigma on the family of her parents. In South Asian societies, the life of a divorcee is especially difficult. Unlike Western societies, where 'mind your own business' is the order of the day, in South Asian societies everybody seems to be curious about what happens next door. The fear of divorce would make a wife bear the unjust attitude of her husband, make no protest and lead life as a docile pet. Among all these potential problems, one apparently positive point was that finding a match for a girl was not a challenge, as the elders would decide about the match. Such decisions would meet little resistance from the girls because of their 'voiceless' status.

CHANGING TRENDS

With the changing times over the last four decades, two emerging trends could be seen in South Asian societies. First, women started getting exposure to education. This exposure was previously confined to basic religious education at home. Secondly, the society at large became more generous in terms of accepting the role of women and their place in society. The effect of modern urbanization and commercialization weakened family bonds in South Asian societies. This led to a significant decline in the trend of marriages within the families. The factor of women getting higher education and joining the labour force resulted in at least two important outcomes. Girls, who formerly had no say in their marriages, after acquiring higher education became more vocal and selective. Further, because of education and enhanced awareness, there was a decline in the tendency towards early marriages, which started diminishing.

FINDING A MATCH

These two outcomes, which apparently looked positive, created some challenges for the marriage of girls. The biggest challenge that parents would face was difficulty in finding suitable matches for their daughters and sons. Marriages which were decided by elders at an early age within the families or a certain tribe or caste, were no more possible because of enhanced awareness and the regained voice on the part of boys and girls.

MATRIMONIAL ADVERTISEMENTS

Unlike western societies, in South Asian families the responsibility of marrying off their sons and daughters generally lies with the parents or elders of the family. This is more so in the case of daughters, for socio-economic reasons. In the last three decades, one can see an increased number of matrimonial advertisements in the print media and presence of matrimonial services on TV and the Internet. A close study of these matrimonial advertisements reveals some important dimensions of the interplay of language, gender, and power.

The underlying philosophy of all commercial advertising is to make the products attractive for the clients. Matrimonial advertisements are constructed along similar lines. Some of the variable that became relevant to a matrimonial ad were: age, educational qualifications, profession, family/caste, height, workplace/sector, residential area, social status, looks/colour, marital status/second marriage, nationality, family background, religion/sect, income, and children.

ATTRIBUTE OF BEAUTY

The view of an ideal woman was reflected in matrimonial ads. The majority of the advertisements about girls mentions the beauty of the girl. The ads employ the words like *khoobsoorat* (pretty), *bohat khoobsoorat* (extremely pretty), *khoobsoorat tareen* (the prettiest). A number of advertisements further elaborate the notion of beauty by defining it, e.g., fair complexion is a stereotype that defines beauty in South Asian societies. So *gori rangat* (fair complexion) is highlighted in the ads. Some times *teekhe naqsh* (sharp features) are also mentioned as an indicator of beauty.

RELATED ATTRIBUTES OF BEAUTY

Another expectation of society is that women should be tall. This attribute is reflected in a number of advertisements by mentioning the term *tall,* and in some cases the exact measurement of height in terms of feet and inches, is given. A further attribute in such advertisements is *slimness.* In some advertisements, the expression 'slim and smart' is used. Youth is another socially desirable quality and certain ads mention the exact age in numbers to make the proposition attractive. Thus, the description of girls revolves around their physical features, i.e. young, beautiful, tall, slim, and smart.

AGE

Teenage was considered to be the appropriate age for a girl's marriage in South Asian families. But with more social awareness and girls obtaining college and university education, this age has been extended to the late twenties and even the early thirties. Still, age for women is considered to be an important factor. It is important to note that this factor is not considered crucial for men. Society has different sets of expectations from men and from women and in most of the cases these expectations favour men.

PROFESSION

Profession is another factor, especially in the case of boys. A profession is an indicator of economic position. At the same time, it becomes a touchstone for social status. Certain professions which may not have good incomes but carry influence are also considered, e.g., a job in the police or in income tax. In the case of girls, profession was not a relevant attribute in the past. Even some educated girls would not take jobs. But the trend is changing now. Enhanced social awareness, together with increasing economic compulsions, have prompted women to work. Thus, we see mention of their professions in the matrimonial ads about women.

GOOD MANNERS

In case of girls, it is considered important that they should be *sugghar* (well mannered) and adept in household matters, i.e. cooking, washing clothes, etc. This stereotypical expectation is visible in the matrimonial ads. As mentioned earlier, in South Asian societies it is not just the husband but other members of husband's family may constantly monitor and judge the bride's conduct. It is therefore considered mandatory for the girl to have good manners and to be respectful and obedient.

EDUCATIONAL QUALIFICATION

Besides the physical features of girls, there is also a mention of education which is considered to be important because, if the girl is educated, she could do a job and could be helpful in running the family. Sometimes the names of prestigious educational organizations are also mentioned to further enhance the impact of the advertisement, e.g., MBBS from King Edward Medical College, etc.

NATIONALITY

An interesting phenomenon that became significant in South Asian societies is the fact of settlement in developed countries like the USA, UK, Australia, etc. This would not only indicate the economic stability of the candidate but would ensure a higher socio-economic position of the individual in the society. Beside economic stability and social status, this factor would also mean that there is less likelihood that the bride would be living in a joint family system. With all its positive points, this variable started appearing in the ads quite recently. Presumably, the possession of an American residence card or Canadian or Australian immigration would give an individual substantial edge over other candidates.

FAMILY BACKGROUND

Keeping in view the close-knit families in South Asian societies, it is not the marriage of a boy and girl but a relationship between two families. Thus girl's family, their social class, their status and relatives become important. One may find complimentary expressions written about the family, e.g., 'small family'. The mention of small family, at times, is crucial as a large family means more responsibilities and liabilities. Sometimes the father's profession is mentioned, e.g., father is a doctor, or engineer. In one advertisement it was mentioned that the father of the girl was a 'grade twenty officer'. In a few ads it was mentioned that the family is 'highly influential, highly placed'.

LOCATION/RESIDENTIAL AREA

An indicator of socio-economic status is the residential area in which the candidate resides. In an indirect manner, this factor helps determine the 'class' and status of the family. In some ads, a point was made to mention the 'posh area' where the girl's family resides. This indicator points to the socio-economic status of the family.

Religion/Caste/Denomination

Religious affiliations are also considered important. Apart from major denominations, some further sects are also mentioned. Similarly, language and castes, in some cases, are considered crucial. All these cultural expressions are constituents of identity at individual and community level. The caste factor, which used to be a compelling factor in the past, has weakened over time because of the spread of education and enhanced social awareness.

Advertisements in Pakistani Newspapers

To understand the trends in the matrimonial ads, a sample of 431 adverts was collected during the periods of March, April, and May 2009. Among them 217 advertisements were for males seeking females and 214 advertisements were females seeking males. These ads were collected from four Pakistani newspapers including *Dawn*, *The News* (English newspapers), *Nawa-i-Waqt*, and *Jang* (Urdu newspapers). The distribution of advertisements can be seen in the following table.

Table 10.2: Sample Distribution

Jang		Nawa-i-Waqt		Dawn		The News	
M	F	M	F	M	F	M	F
54	62	57	46	53	53	53	53

Table 10.3 tabulates the attributes found in the matrimonial ads given by male candidates.

Table 10.3: Male seeking suitors

Variable	Percentage	Variable	Percentage
Age	96	Looks/Colour	28
Qualification	75	Marital Status/Second Marriage	24
Profession	63	Nationality	24
Family/Caste	48	Family Background	23
Height	44	Religion/Sect	22
Work place/Sector	36	Other	18
Residential Area	34	Income	11
Social Status	33	Children	5

Let us examine the attributes mentioned in the advertisements by male candidates. The top attribute in the aggregated score of fours newspapers is 'age', which emerges as the top attribute (96 per cent), followed by 'qualifications' (75 per cent), 'profession' (63 per cent), 'family/caste' (48 per cent), and 'height' (44 per cent). It is interesting to note that age has always been an important attribute in the marriage. 'Qualifications' emerged as a powerful attribute showing its significance in contemporary times. Qualifications may reveal about the socio-economic status of a person with likelihood of greater economic prospects. The third attribute, 'profession', could be an indicator of economic status and social prestige attached to it. 'Family/caste', though at number four, is still a strong attribute in marriage. The 'family/caste' attribute is more specific to those South Asian countries where in certain families marriage outside the 'caste' is discouraged. The attribute of 'height' came at number 5 in male advertisements.

FEMALES SEEKING SUITORS IN PAKISTAN

In the case of female candidates, 214 advertisements from four newspapers were studied. The attributes found can be seen in the following table:

Table 10.4: Attributes in female ads

Variable	Percentage	Variable	Percentage
Age	99	Religion/Sect	26
Qualification	84	Residential Area	23
Height	59	Other	21
Looks/Colour	57	Marital Status/Second Marriage	21
Family/Caste	50	Nationality	14
Family Background	39	Work place/Sector	8
Social Status	37	Children	7
Profession	32	Income	0

Age Factor

The 'age' attribute figured as number one (99 per cent). It is significant that 'age' also emerged as the top attribute in the advertisements of male candidates (96 per cent). The percentage though is higher in the case of female candidates, suggesting that age is more important in the case of women in South Asian societies and the 'youth' factor seems to be more applicable to women rather than men. The attribute of 'qualifications' (84 per cent) is at number 2, as in the case of male ads (75 per cent). It is important to notice that there is a growing realization on the part of women that education is an empowering tool that opens up job prospects and ultimately could lead to economic stability. The attribute of 'height' (59 per cent) is at number three, whereas in case of ads for male candidates this attribute was down at number five (44 per cent).

Looks

The attribute of 'looks/colour' is at number 4, with a score of 57 per cent which is close to the number three attribute 'height' (59 per cent). This attribute, which is at number four in the ads of female candidates drops down to the number 9 (28 per cent) in the ads for male candidates, clearly indicating that the attribute of 'looks' is a stereotypical socially desirable attribute expected from women.

Family

The family/caste factor in ads for female candidates came at number five (50 per cent), whereas in case of ads for male candidates this attribute was at number four (44 per cent), suggesting that this attribute is considered important in both the cases.

Table 10.5: Top Five Attributes in Matrimonial Ads in Pakistan

	Male	Female
1	Age	Age
2	Qualification	Qualification
3	**Profession**	Height
4	Family/Caste	**Looks**
5	Height	Family/Caste

In the above table is a summary of the top five attributes in the ads of male and female candidates. The 'age' is a number one attribute in both male and female ads. Similarly, qualification is at number two. This is important in case of female candidates as educational opportunities were far less available for females in past years. It suggests the rising trend in female education. This finding can be corroborated by the increasing number of ratio of women in higher education. Family/caste is at number four in case of male and at number five in case of females. Similarly, the attribute of height is at number 3 in the case of females and at number five in case of males.

GENDER SPECIFIC ATTRIBUTES

This means that four common attributes, although in a different order, figure among the top five attributes in the ads of males and females. There is, however, one attribute in each group that is specific to it. In the case of males, it is the attribute of *profession* that figures at number three but is absent in the top five attributes of female ads. This suggests that the traditional role of male as a bread earner is still very strong. Women, although catching up on the educational front, are not very conspicuous in term of their presence on the job market. The attribute of *profession* comes at number eight in the female ads. Similarly, in female ads, the attribute of *looks* is at number four, whereas it is absent in the top five attributes of male candidates. This is an important finding that reveals that *profession* plays an important role in describing a man and the attribute of *looks* is crucial in the description of females.

THE EMERGING ATTRIBUTES

There are some attributes that are coming more into the spotlight with the changing times. *Workplace/sector* is mentioned in the male ads (36 per cent) but it has a much lower percentage (8 per cent) in female ads. This is an important observation especially when the *qualification* attribute is at number two position in both the groups. One interpretation could be that a large number of females, even after acquiring higher education, do not join the work force for social and cultural reasons.

MATRIMONIAL ADS IN INDIA

A relatively small sample of fifty ads of female candidates was collected from electronic sites. Ads were retrieved on 23 November 2009 from the following sites:

http://www.advertisementindia.com/Matrimonial-Sample-Advertisements.asp

http://www.hitavadaonline.com/matrimonial.htm

http://www.thehindumatrimonial.com/

The attributes found in the ads can be seen in the following table:

Table 10.6: Females seeking suitors in India

Variable	Percentage	Variable	Percentage
Age	96	Family Background	32
Family/Caste	82	Residential Area	28
Height	82	Social Status	18
Qualification	76	Marital Status/Second Marriage	14
Religion/Sect	60	Other	10
Looks/Colour	56	Income	8
Profession	42	Nationality	6
Work place/Sector	38	Children	2

It is important to observe that age remains the top attribute in India as well. Family/caste and height with the same score are at number two. Qualification is at number three. Religion is at number four and looks/colour is at number five. It is interesting to note that four attributes age, family/caste, height, and looks/colour are common with the top five attributes found in Pakistani female ads. The attribute of religion is the one that is present in the female ads in India but is absent in Pakistan. A plausible explanation for this could be that an overwhelming majority of the Pakistani population is Muslim whereas in India there is a greater diversity of religions. Thus, in the Indian context, the attribute of religion can be an important piece of information required in match-making.

MATRIMONIAL ADS IN SRI LANKA

A sample of fifty matrimonial ads were taken from *Sunday Observer*. The information was retrieved on 22 March 2009, Sunday 29 March 2009 (http://www.sundayobserver.lk). The attributes found can be seen in the following table.

Table 10.7: Females seeking suitors in Sri Lanka

Variable	Percentage	Variable	Percentage
Age	98	Residential Area	46
Looks/Colour	78	Social Status	46
Profession	74	Other	26
Family/Caste	72	Family Background	24
Qualification	72	Marital Status/Second Marriage	22
Height	68	Nationality	20
Religion/Sect	66	Children	6
Work place/Sector	52	Salary	2

The following table compares the top five attributes found in the ads for female candidates in three South Asian countries:

Table 10.8: Top Five Attributes in Female ads in Pakistan, India, and Sri Lanka

Rank	Pakistan	%	India	%	Sri Lanka	%
1	Age	99	Age	96	Age	98
2	Qualification	84	Family/Caste	82	Looks/Colour	78
3	Height	59	Height	82	Profession	74
4	Looks/Colour	57	Qualification	76	Family/Caste	72
5	Family/Caste	50	Religion/Sect	60	Qualification	72

FEMALE MATRIMONIAL ADS

Age remains the top factor in Sri Lanka, as in case of Indian and Pakistani female ads. Similarly, family/caste, height, and qualification are among the top five attributes, as in the case of Indian and Pakistani matrimonial ads for female candidates. The only attribute which is specific to Sri Lankan women is the attribute of 'Profession' that appears as the number three attribute. The appearance of this attribute among the top five attributes indicates that a large number of Sri Lankan women do become a part of the labour force. It could be because of the socio-cultural norms of the country or/and because of the very high literacy rate of Sri Lanka, which is much higher than that of India or of Pakistan.

Matrimonial ads, which are relatively a recent phenomenon in South Asia, grew in volume for a number of reasons, including more education and greater awareness among girls, weakening trend of marriage within families, and girls finding their voice to select or reject a candidate. This led to a sharp decrease in early marriages but at the same time created new challenges, especially for girls to find suitable boys. Keeping in view the wide and fast access to media, people found it an effective source to tap the potential candidate through matrimonial ads in the newspapers. The study of these ads on the one hand shows how societal stereotypes are reflected in these ads, and on the other hand suggest that such widely circulated articles are in fact further perpetuating the gendered expectations of society.

PART 4

LANGUAGE, GENDER, AND EDUCATION

Chapter 11
Gender and Education

The school shapes the consciousness and behaviour of the students by distributing the cultural practices of the dominant groups as the norm. Students who acquired this linguistic and cultural capital would grow to justify and serve the interests of the dominant groups.

– Suresh Canagarajah

She is defined and differentiated with reference to man and not he with reference to her; she is the incidental, the inessential as opposed to the essential. He is the Subject, he is the Absolute—she is the Other.

– Simone de Beauvoir

Gender is a political view of sex that is based on the binary division between male and female. This binary division apparently looks natural. The problem, however, begins when one part is considered inferior and the other superior. Meanings are given arbitrarily to the objects and notions. Apart from literal or dictionary meanings, each word has a certain connotation or associated meaning. This part of meaning is constructed by society. The dominant groups of a society assign positive meanings to what they do and negative meanings to what 'others' do.

VALIDATION OF STEREOTYPES

The construction of gender is largely done by the dominant groups by assigning roles and responsibilities, expectations, and opportunities for males and females separately. For instance, it is society that suggests girls should play with dolls only and boys cannot (and should not) play with dolls. In this process of socialization, education and educational institutions play a central role. For instance, stereotypes about the responsibilities, roles, and opportunities, to which we are initially exposed in family settings, become authenticated through the educational institutions. Thus, schools are places where the socialising process becomes more effective in terms of legitimacy and authenticity. The social knowledge relating to gender is constructed, validated, and perpetuated in schools in the form of textbooks, pedagogy, assessment, and the school milieu.

Before we look at the historic trends in female education in South Asia, it is important to examine the demographic composition of the population. Surprisingly, unlike in the rest of the world, the proportion of females is less than that of males in South Asia, which has one of the most peculiar sex ratios in the world. According to Nanda and Jagtdeb (2008: 15–16), 'Excluding South Asia, the ratio of females to males in the world is 106–100: in South Asia it is only 94 to 100, a discrepancy suggesting that 75 million women are simply "missing"—either not allowed to be born, dead of chronic malnutrition, or having never received any medical care.'

FEMALE EDUCATION IN UNITED INDIA

If we trace the history of female education in the former united India, we do not come across many initiatives in terms of modern education that could help women obtain jobs. On the other hand, we see opposition to such educational initiatives on socio-cultural pretexts. One school of thought did not approve of any kind of education for girls. The other school of thought permitted only rudimentary religious education for girls. Modern education was considered injurious for women. In one of the most popular books written for women, *Bahishti Zevar* (Heavenly Ornament), Thanvi (1997: 78–79) suggested that,

Only men need to do a job since men are responsible for the livelihood of women. Since women need to observe *pardah* (taking the veil), job-related knowledge cannot be acquired by them. Thus, this kind of education is useless for women and just a waste of time; rather, it is hazardous for women.

SOCIO-CULTURAL CONSTRAINTS

This denial of education for women was less due to religious reasons and more because of the socio cultural milieu of united India, where women were mostly confined to the household. After the partition of 1947, we see a number of institutions for women in India and Pakistan. The Report of the Commission on National Education (1959: 189) recommended that, 'It is essential that the foundation of education for women be firmly consolidated and that the facilities available for girls' education be in every respect equal to those available for boys'. This proposal was not taken in its true spirit as most of the reform plans for the betterment of female education in Pakistan focused on numbers.

A number of donor-funded projects have been aimed at enhancing the literacy rate. This quantitative approach served well for the end-of-project reports, to demonstrate the impact with increased numbers. But, since the problem is deeply rooted, merely enhancing numbers cannot remove it. The current literacy rate in Pakistan suggests that there remains a huge gap between male and female literacy rates. The reasons for the relatively low female literacy rate are many, including, for example, poverty, lack of awareness, socio-cultural taboos, and location of schools in far-flung areas or in an unsafe environment.

QUANTITATIVE EXPANSION OF FEMALE LITERACY

Quantitative expansion, which has been the focus of most of the funded projects by multinational donors, is important but mere enhanced numbers cannot resolve the deep-rooted problem of gender disparity in society. It's the qualitative aspect which needs to be addressed. The Begum of Bhopal, quoted in Khan (1999: 39), observed: 'It is a stupid thing, to my mind, to teach the girls to read and write, and then leave them to their fate. The very least that should be done for them, is to give them a thorough grounding in things that matter, and to awaken the dormant soul in them.' There has been an increase in the number of educational institutions for boys and girls in the last five decades. Among these institutions, some are qualitatively superior to others. This difference has been further widened with the advent of private schools. A large number of girls does have access to school but the quality of these educational institutions is the real question. Mansoor et al., (2007: 156) report in a research study that, 'In private schools, including junior schools, where the medium of instruction is English, boys are more likely to attend these private schools. Parents are reluctant to send their daughters to these schools because most of them are co-educational.'

GENDER REPRESENTATION

Research done on textbooks shows that representation of female characters in textbooks showed them as weak, dependent, stereotypical, shy, and confined to the home, whereas male characters are shown as strong, independent, innovative, outgoing, and responsible for the outer world. The authenticity of the printed word in the shape of a textbook is further enhanced when these stereotypes are backed up and legitimized by the teacher in the class. The assessment system approves of certain agreed upon answers and disapproves nonconformity with the fixed stereotypes. The school milieu also plays an important part in the formation and perpetuation of certain gender stereotypes. The schools thus are playing an important part in the dissemination of stereotypes favouring the patriarchal system in society.

CLASSROOM DYNAMICS

Once they manage to enter a school, the girls are exposed to gender biased books. In the recent past there have been some attempts to purge the textbooks of sexist material. But the real curriculum happens in class where the teacher's everyday actions and utterances construct the curricula. There is a common observation that in a co-education class the boys tend to engage teachers in an aggressive manner in terms of participation.

EDUCATION AND POWER

Education, which has a strong linkage with power, has been a rare commodity for women. In Pakistan, we see a long period of exclusion of women in terms of modern education. That is why women had to struggle hard to compete with men and make their way forward. Still, in certain parts of India and Pakistan girls' exposure has been confined to only rudimentary religious education and modern education, which is a potential key to economic independence, is denied to them. The control and hegemony enjoyed by men is largely linked with their role as bread earners of the family. Economic independence is generally ensured by the acquisition of modern education.

SCHOOLS AND GENDER STEREOTYPES

Educational institutions have been engaged in perpetuating the existing social structures of power through construction and legitimization of skewed view about women. For instance, there are fixed beliefs about women that they are not very good at science subjects. Halai (2007: 123) refers to this mindset:

> Boys are favoured in Mathematics classrooms in Pakistan, in terms of the teaching approaches used, content and layout of the curriculum and the teachers' perceptions of boys as better mathematicians.

Continued gender disparity in Mathematics classrooms means that girls are denied the opportunity to engage in a positive manner with Mathematics.

INTERNALIZATION OF STEREOTYPES

Even the female students are led to internalize gender biased views against them in schools. Thus, education, which is supposed to emancipate human beings, is ironically performing the opposite function by creating tunnel vision among the students. This tunnel vision is designed to favour the powerful and discredit the marginalized groups. If we are serious in reducing the gender gaps in the society, we need to revisit some of the popular stereotypes about women. For this, social institutions in general and schools in particular have to play their role. We need to have a thorough review of textbooks, pedagogy, assessment systems, and school milieu, and address the areas of improvement.

CLASSROOM AND GENDER CONSTRUCTION

Classrooms are important places where certain gender stereotypes are validated and perpetuated. Teachers' discourse and actions may approve the gendered behaviour at conscious or unconscious levels. Education, which is supposed to broaden the intellectual horizons of children and lead them to emancipation and freedom, seems to fail in its fundamental objective. Gender stereotypes, which need to be challenged in schools, are in fact further strengthened in the dynamics of teaching and learning. The current notion of education is generally the obtaining of a certificate or degree to be eligible to get a job on the market. The real function of education, which is to develop critical thinking skills in order to bring a change at the individual and societal levels, is either ignored or underestimated.

CHALLENGING STEREOTYPES

Challenging gender stereotypes in term of roles, expectations, and opportunities, is not only crucial for boys but also for girls. For boys, it is important to see that most of the gender stereotypes are based on myths and there is no scientific basis for male superiority. On the other hand, girls, who are the target of these stereotypes, come under their influence through 'spontaneous consent'. It is important for girls to come out of the illusion of an artificially created world where they find themselves helpless. Education in its essence should aim at enhancing the choices and opportunities at the personal and public levels by challenging stereotypes regarding women in terms of their roles and expectations. According to Bhasin (2008: 203), 'We have to strengthen and multiply not only those ongoing efforts to educate women but also acquire information and knowledge which helps challenge patriarchal knowledge, norms, values and behaviour patterns.'

CHANGING TIMES

In a large number of families of the subcontinent, it is still believed that there is no need to send girls to school. Similarly, a sizable portion of the population believes that girls should only be exposed to primary education. The argument given in favour is that, since girls need to be married off, there is no need to send them for higher education. This situation is changing and we can see an increasing number of girls joining schools and colleges. But one problem that still exists is that a number of female professionals, i.e. medical doctors, engineers, etc., after successful completion of their professional degrees, do not work. One major reason is their marriage. After the marriage, they find it genuinely difficult to practice their professions. In most such cases, it is because they are not *allowed* by their husbands to work. As discussed earlier, women and men are viewed by society through the lens of gender, in which man is considered responsible for the outer world and a woman's role has been confined to the home.

UNDER-UTILIZATION OF POTENTIAL

This poses a relevant question to the validity of an education which has not been able to bring any change with reference to the roles of men and women in society. It suggests that there is something lacking in the kind of education our schools are providing to our young generation. The missing part is the critical thinking that requires the learners to raise questions, look for the alternatives, transform their lives, and ultimately their society. Thus, as we emphasise quantitative enhancement in the female literacy rate, we should be cognizant of the fact that education per se is not empowerment as it is not increasing the girls' chances of a better life and transforming their status in terms of their roles, expectations, and opportunities. If we are interested in real change, we need to be concerned about the quality of education and plan to improve it in a systematic manner.

GENDER AS PRACTICE

While we strategize to reduce the gender gaps in society, it is crucial to keep in view that gender is not just an idea or a notion which should be dealt with only at a theoretical level. Gender, besides an idea, is every day practice. (Austin, 1962; Butler, 1990, 1993). In our social interactions, through our attitudes and practices, we make gender happen. So, the strategy should not be confined to theory only but should be reflected in our daily life practice. For instance, it is not sufficient to include the gender equality notions in the curriculum but it is crucial that teachers and head teachers should show with their practice that they firmly believe in gender equality. Educational institutions are alleged to perpetuate gender-biased stereotypes but it is the same educational institutions that can prepare students to challenge these stereotypes and put up resistance to the hegemonic designs of dominant groups. What is required from our educational institutions is that they expose students to the socio-political aspects of language. This needs a shift from purely *technical* teaching to *critical pedagogy* that should help students realize the important role of language in the construction of social reality. There is a need to create awareness among students regarding the role language can play in the politics of representation.

Chapter 12
Nursery Rhymes and Gender Representation

According to gender schema theory, when the culture (language, art, customs, economy, polity, etc.) is stereotyped according to gender, children become gender schematic without even realizing it. They develop networks of associations that guide their perceptions, so that they come to see the world in gender-polarized ways.

– Scott Coltrane

The power of convention, or custom, lies in the fact that we simply learn ways of being and ways of doing things without considering any reasons behind them, and without recognizing the larger structure that they fall into.

– Eckert and McConnell-Ginet

School is an important social institution but even before school the family acts as a potent social institution that constructs gender realities through language use. Gender stereotypes are engraved into children's minds at an early age through nursery rhymes and fairy tales. Mo and Shen (2002: 131) suggest that, 'If parents are children's first teachers, nursery rhymes should be considered as their first literacy-learning materials.'

MOTHER GOOSE

There are a number of anthologies of nursery rhymes available on market but the most popular is the *Mother Goose* anthology. *Mother Goose* was first published in 1916. Its popularity prompted imitation of the real *Mother Goose* in other parts of the world. *The Real Mother Goose* contains 305 rhymes. Most of these poems, apparently funny, perpetuate some and authenticate other gender stereotypes. This chapter focuses on some popular nursery rhymes selected from *Mother Goose*.

In some rhymes, we see the conspicuous exclusion of women as is the practice in many social activities. Look at the scenario depicted in the following rhyme (Wright, 1994: 55), where the Lord Mayor is sitting with his men in the presence of a cock, a hen and chickens.

Forehead, Eyes, Cheeks, Nose, Mouth, and Chin

Here sits the Lord Mayor,
Here sit his two men,
Here sits the cock,
Here sits the hen,
Here sit the little chickens,
Here they run in.
Chin-chopper, chin-chopper, chin-chopper, chin!

Beauty appears to be the most wanted attribute in the world of rhymes and fairy tales. The concept of a heroine in the rhymes is incomplete if she is not pretty. A popular stereotype is that all women are desperate for words of appreciation, especially appreciation of their beauty. One of the traditional attributes of beauty is fair colour. In this rhyme (Wright, 1994: 66), a quick recipe is shared to have a permanent fair colour.

The First of May

The fair maid who, the first of May,
Goes to the fields at break of day,
And washes in dew from the hawthorn-tree,
Will ever after handsome be.

Here is another poem (Wright, 1994: 41), where an old woman is hard of hearing but gets the pleasant message without any difficulty.

Shall We Go A-Shearing?

'Old woman, old woman, shall we go a-shearing?'
'Speak a little louder, sir, I am very thick of hearing.'
'Old woman, old woman, shall I kiss you dearly?'
'Thank you, kind sir, I hear you very clearly.'

It is interesting to note that a number of rhymes refer to the image of an 'old woman'. Some rhymes that talk about the old woman include *Dame Trot and Her Cat*, *The Old Woman under a Hill*, *Oh, Dear! Old Mother Goose*, *A Needle and Thread*, *Goosey Goosey Gander*, *Old Mother Hubbard*, *The Old Woman from France*, *A Strange Old Woman*, *The Hobby-Horse*, *Old Woman, Old Woman*, *The Old Woman and the Pedlar*, *There was an Old Woman who Lived in a Shoe*, *The Three Sons*, *The Old Woman of Leeds*, *The Old Woman of Harrow That's All*, *There was an Old Woman*, and *The Woman of Exeter*. These old women are leading miserable, isolated lives, cut off from a society that is not concerned about them. It is important to note that because of more cohesive family bonds old people in South Asian families remain part of the homes and are not left alone. One left-out woman is described in the following rhyme (Wright, 1992: 13):

The Old Woman under a Hill

There was an old woman
Lived under a hill;
And if she's not gone,
She lives there still.

Language, according to Hussein (2004: 117), 'is used to produce and reproduce cultural experiences. As a social and cultural phenomenon, it is used to communicate about every aspect of cultural experience in a society.' The stereotype that women are talkative is further perpetuated through nursery rhymes. In the following rhyme (Wright, 1992: 57), we see an old woman who is never 'quiet':

A Strange Old Woman

There was an old woman, and what do you think?
She lived upon nothing but victuals, and drink;
Victuals and drink were the chief of her diet,
And yet this old woman could never be quiet.

Gender, being a social construct, assigns the responsibility of the outside to men and the domestic chores to women. This division of labour can be seen in the following rhyme (Wright, 1992: 76):

My Maid Mary

My maid Mary she minds the dairy,
While I go a-hoeing and mowing each morn;
Gaily run the reel and the little spinning wheel,
While I am singing and mowing my corn.

This makes women entirely dependent on men. Here is a rhyme (Wright, 1994: 21) that ends with an anticlimax as pragmatic needs shatter the fantasy dreams:

A Man and a Maid

There was a little man,
Who wooed a little maid,
And he said, 'Little maid, will you wed, wed, wed?
I have little more to say,
So will you, yea or nay,
For least said is soonest mended-ded, ded, ded.'

The little maid replied,
'Should I be your little bride,
Pray what must we have for to eat, eat, eat?
Will the flame that you're so rich in,
Light a fire in the kitchen?
Or the little god of love turn the spit, spit, spit?'

Here is a similar rhyme (Wright, 1994: 112) that ends on an unhappy note as the beauty of the girl is suppressed by her poverty and the boy changes his mind:

Where Are You Going My Pretty Maid

'Where are you going, my pretty maid?'
'I'm going a-milking, sir,' she said.
'May I go with you, my pretty maid?'
'You're kindly welcome, sir,' she said.
'What is your father, my pretty maid?'
'My father's a farmer, sir,' she said.
'What is your fortune, my pretty maid?'
'My face is my fortune, sir,' she said.
'Then I can't marry you, my pretty maid.'
'Nobody asked you, sir,' she said.

It is important to note that in the fairy tales and the rhymes where there are no male characters the family is in a poor condition and life becomes harder for a woman. In the nursery rhyme given below (Wright, 1994: 116), there is an old woman who has 'many children' but she does not have a house to live in and thus lives in a big shoe. They are so poor, as there is no male breadwinner in the house, and the mother gives her children broth without bread.

There was an Old Woman who Lived in a Shoe

There was an old woman who lived in a shoe.
She had so many children, she didn't know what to do.
She gave them some broth,
Without any bread,
Whipped them all soundly, and sent them to bed.

In *Dance to your Daddie* (Wright, 1994: 50), we see that a small family is waiting for the male member, who has gone fishing to come and bring some fish to eat. The mother is promising her daughter that, 'You shall get a fishy, when the boat comes home.'

Dance to your Daddie

Dance to your daddie,
My bonnie laddie;
Dance to your daddie, my bonnie lamb;
You shall get a fishy,
On a little dishy;
You shall get a fishy, when the boat comes home.

Here, male characters being presented as physically strong and in possession of economic resources are in a relatively much better position to raise their offspring. In the following rhyme (Wright, 1994: 41), one can see the difference between a dove and a wren in terms of taking care of their offspring.

The Dove and the Wren

The dove says coo, coo, what shall I do?
I can scarce maintain two.
Pooh, pooh! says the wren, I've got ten,
And keep them all like gentlemen.

In another rhyme, *Fingers and Toes* (Wright, 1994: 12), women are presented as strange creatures who appear to be abnormal.

Fingers and Toes

Every lady in this land
Has twenty nails, upon each hand
Five, and twenty on hands and feet:
All this is true, without deceit.

The abnormal appearance is also associated with grotesque deeds. Here is a woman who starts with spinning and resorts to some inexplicable actions (Wright, 1994: 100):

That's All

There was an old woman sat spinning,
And that's the first beginning;
She had a calf,
And that's half;
She took it by the tail,
And threw it over the wall,
And that's all!

The politics of categorization and labelling can be seen in some nursery rhymes. The following rhyme (Wright, 1994: 83) talks about the experience with a particular woman and then stereotypes this experience by generalizing it for all the women:

Dapple-Gray

I had a little pony,
His name was Dapple-Gray,
I lent him to a lady,
To ride a mile away.
She whipped him, she slashed him,
She rode him through the mire;
I would not lend my pony now
For all the lady's hire.

Women are also presented as bizarre characters. This caricature presentation can be seen in the following rhyme (Wright, 1994: 16). It is important to observe that wives are bracketed with other subhuman items like 'kits, cats, and sacks'.

Going To St. Ives

As I was going to St. Ives,
I met a man with seven wives.
Every wife had seven sacks,
Every sack had seven cats,
Every cat had seven kits.
Kits, cats, sacks, and wives,
How many were going to St. Ives?

A common stereotype is that women are tentative and confused and lack confidence. Such stereotypes have no scientific basis but are perpetuated through different media, such as sayings and proverbs, jokes, songs, fairy tales, and nursery rhymes. Below is such a nursery rhyme that perpetuates this stereotype (Wright, 1994: 71). The rhyme is about an old woman who is unable to recognize herself because of changes in her clothes.

The Old Woman and the Pedlar

There was an old woman, as I've heard tell,
She went to market her eggs for to sell;
She went to market all on a market-day,
And she fell asleep on the King's highway.

There came by a pedlar whose name was Stout,
He cut her petticoats all round about;
He cut her petticoats up to the knees,
Which made the old woman to shiver and freeze.
When the little old woman first did wake,
She began to shiver and she began to shake;
She began to wonder and she began to cry,
'Lauk a mercy on me, this can't be I!

'But if I be I, as I hope it be,
I've a little dog at home, and he'll know me;
If it be I, he'll wag his little tail,
And if it be not I, he'll loudly bark and wail.'
Home went the little woman all in the dark;
Up got the little dog, and he began to bark;
He began to bark, so she began to cry,
'Lauk a mercy on me, this is none of I!'

One of the common gender stereotypes is that females are cowards (Wright, 1994: 39). Even very small things can frighten them and make them cry.

Little Miss Muffet

Little Miss Muffet, sat on a tuffet,
Eating her curds and whey;
Along came a spider,
Who sat down beside her,
And frightened Miss Muffet away.

Women are generally considered shopaholics, who love dresses and related items. This stereotype is reflected in the following rhyme (Wright, 1994: 127). As the rhyme opens, we see a female character showing her worry because Johnny has not come back from a fair. She repeats the lines, 'What can the matter be?' followed by the line, 'He promised to buy me a bunch of blue ribbons'. This line, with slight variation, repeated three times, reveals the real cause for concern.

The Bunch of Blue Ribbons

Oh, dear, what can the matter be?
Dear, dear, what can the matter be?
Oh, dear, what can the matter be?
Johnny's so long at the fair.
He promised to buy me a bunch of blue ribbons;
He promised to buy me some bonny blue ribbons;
He promised to buy me a bunch of blue ribbons,
To bind up my bonny brown hair.
And it's, oh! Dear! What can the matter be?
Dear, dear, what can the matter be?
Oh, dear, what can the matter be?
Johnny's so long at the fair.

Nursery rhymes appear to be an effective means of manufacturing gender roles and power positions in society. The following nursery rhyme (Wright, 1994: 107) is woven around playing cards, using the characters of king, queen and knave. It is interesting to examine the role of each character. The queen is given a stereotypical role of cooking and she makes tarts. But she is so weak that she cannot stop the knave from stealing the tarts. Ultimately, the king emerges in the story as a saviour who beats the knave, brings back the tarts and rescues the queen from an untoward situation.

The Tarts

The Queen of Hearts,
She made some tarts,
All on a summer's day;
The Knave of Hearts,
He stole the tarts,
And took them clean away.
The King of Hearts
Called for the tarts,
And beat the Knave full sore;
The Knave of Hearts
Brought back the tarts,
And vowed he'd steal no more.

The image of a male character as saviour is very common in children's fairy tales and rhymes. Male characters are presented as symbols of strength, who can exert power and create an impact. The climax of the following rhyme (Wright, 1994: 53) refers to such potential act.

If all the Seas were One Sea

If all the seas were one sea,
What a great sea that would be!
And if all the trees were one tree,
What a great tree that would be!
And if all the axes were one axe,
What a great axe that would be!
And if all the men were one man,
What a great man he would be!
And if the great man took the great axe,

And cut down the great tree,
And let it fall into the great sea,
What a splish splash that would be!

The male characters are presented as dominant and confident, not only physically strong but possessing the resolve to realize their dreams. One such character is presented in the following poem (Wright, 1994: 73):

One, He Loves

One, he loves; two, he loves;
Three, he loves, they say;
Four, he loves with all his heart;
Five, he casts away.
Six, he loves; seven, she loves;
Eight, they both love.
Nine, he comes; ten, he tarries;
Eleven, he courts; twelve, he marries.

We also find marriages of convenience in nursery rhymes. A person with money in his pocket claims to buy his wife. This shows that poverty stricken families would sell their daughter for a good price (Wright, 1994: 118).

When

When I was a bachelor,
I lived by myself;
And all the bread and cheese I got,
I laid up on the shelf.

The rats and the mice,
They made such a strife,
I was forced to go to London,
To buy me a wife.

The streets were so bad,
And the lanes were so narrow,

I was forced to bring my wife home,
In a wheelbarrow.
The wheelbarrow broke,
And my wife had a fall;
Down came wheelbarrow,
Little wife and all.

The assigning of roles is decided by society at a very early age. Girls and boys are associated with different toys and different sports. With these toys and sports are associated the future roles they are supposed to play in their real lives. Girls play with dolls and take good care of them, as they are supposed to do with their babies later in their lives. This early training is evident in the following rhyme (Wright, 1994: 17):

Baby Dolly

Hush, baby, my dolly, I pray you don't cry,
And I'll give you some bread, and some milk by-and-by;
Or perhaps you like custard, or, maybe, a tart,
Then to either you're welcome, with all my heart.

Similar feelings are depicted in a fantasy rhyme, where a woman is thinking about her husband and the manner she would take care of him (Wright, 1994: 57).

I had a Little Husband

I had a little husband no bigger than my thumb,
I put him in a pint pot, and there I bid him drum,
I bought a little handkerchief to wipe his little nose,
And a pair of little garters to tie his little hose.

These nursery rhymes depict a certain age and context that were remote from South Asia. However, we see points of similarity. According to D'Souza (2005: 101) '. . . there is one thing that is common to these rhymes and to Indian society of today—the stereotypes of patriarchy, which assign rigid gender-based roles to boys and girls right from their childhood.' Nursery rhymes, imported from foreign countries, have been used in a number of schools in South Asia. They perpetuate some serious gendered stereotypes in an apparently playful manner. Children easily memorize these short and simple rhymes. The more the rhymes are repeated, the stronger is the effect of communicated stereotypes.

Chapter 13
Representation of Women in Fairy Tales

Not very long after she had a daughter, with skin as white as snow, lips as red as blood, and hair as black as ebony.

– Snow White

. . . thou canst not release them but by being dumb for seven years: thou must neither speak nor laugh; and wert thou to speak one single word, and it wanted but one hour of the seven years, all would be in vain, and thy brothers would perish because of that one word.

– The Twelve Brothers

Gender is a social construct that is manufactured by various social institutions. It is actually performed in a society on regular basis (Butler, 1990). The society makes up gender by determining roles, expectations, and opportunities for males and females on the basis of sex (Goddard and Patterson, 2000).

The process of manufacturing gender starts even before children go to school. The family plays a vital role in shaping the self-image and identity of boys and girls. Fairy tales also play an important role in the gender construction process. Story telling is a common phenomenon in most societies. Children are exposed to stories at home and in initial classes at school, as a part of educational activities. According to Wallowitz (2004: 28), folk tales 'serve several important functions in a society that include projecting values and expressing a culture's taboos and anxieties.'

LISTENING AND READING EXPOSURE

Children love to listen to stories and also enjoy reading colourful story books, which take them into the world of fantasy and imagination. Some serious messages become imprinted on their minds in a subtle manner. Rachlin and Vogt, quoted in Tepper and Cassidy (1999: 265), suggest: 'Books may help provide the basic model by which children form ideas about themselves as well as about other people'. These initial impressions about gender remain with them for a long time.

Grimm's Fairy Tales

The sample for this research comprised 211 fairy tales contained in the book, *Grimm's Fairy Tales* (2000). The book was compiled by Jacob and Wilhelm Grimm. Its first volume, containing 86 stories, was published in 1812, followed by the second volume in 1814 that contained seventy stories. In the newer editions of the book, certain stories have been added, deleted, or modified. Most of the tales contained in the book have German or French origins. The book is considered to be the most famous collection of fairy tales. Some of these tales are used in a number of countries as part of their syllabi. Similarly, in South Asian schools, students are exposed to these tales as they are used in early classes of English medium schools.

Common Pattern

One can find a common pattern in most of the tales, which consist of an issue, problem, question, challenge, dream or a desire, followed by a journey involving challenges, adventures, calamities, and dangers. The problem is ultimately resolved by a saviour, who usually happens to be a kind, good looking, cooperative, skilful, and brave male character. Going through these stories, one observes that women do not even figure in a number of stories. This exclusion suggests that women were not relevant to the kinds of roles and themes presented in those stories and is a reflection of female exclusion in real society. There are a number of tales, however, where women are present and this chapter focuses on such tales with an attempt to analyse the politics of representation.

GENDER STEREOTYPES

Fairy tales perpetuate certain gender stereotypes in an indirect manner. In most fairy tales, the heroine is a beautiful girl who is sweet and innocent, e.g., *Little Red Riding Hood*, *Cinderella*, *Goldilocks*, *Rumpelstiltskin*, *Sleeping Beauty*, *Snow White*, and *Rapunzel*. The description of the physical features of these women makes them almost unearthly creatures. Here is the description of *Snow White*, 'skin as white as snow, lips as red as blood, and hair as black as ebony.' (Grimm and Grimm, 2000: 330). The king's new wife was proud and overbearing. She used to stand in front of her magic glass (Grimm and Grimm, 2000: 330), look in it, and say:

> 'Looking-glass upon the wall, Who is fairest of us all?'
> And the looking-glass would answer, 'You are fairest of them all.'

Rapunzel was 'the most beautiful child in the world' (Grimm and Grimm, 2000: 94). Her hair, in terms of colour and length, 'shone like gold in the sun and it was so long that it reached from the top of the tower right down to the ground.' In *King Thrushbeard*, the king's daughter was 'beautiful beyond measure' (Grimm and Grimm, 2000: 43). In *The Skilful Huntsman*, '. . . the King's daughter was lying sleeping, and she was so beautiful that he [huntsman] stood still and, holding his breath, looked at her' (Grimm and Grimm, 2000: 72).

FEMININE BEAUTY

In, *The Princess in Disguise*, 'A king once had a wife with golden hair who was so beautiful that none on earth could be found equal to her' (Grimm and Grimm, 2000: 75). In *The Goose-Girl at the Well*, the feminine beauty is described from different perspectives. The physical description is so exaggerated that the female characters emerge as superhuman.

> . . . the youngest of whom [daughters] was so beautiful that the whole world looked on her as a wonder. She was as white as snow, as rosy as apple-blossom, and her hair as radiant as sunbeams. When she cried, not tears fell from her eyes but pearls and jewels only. (Grimm and Grimm, 2000: 281)

Baker-Sperry and Grauerholz (2003: 718) share their findings about the mention of beauty with respect to gender in Table 13.1, which refers to three important findings:

- Women's physical appearance is discussed more frequently than the appearance of male characters.
- Women's beauty is mentioned more frequently than men's handsomeness.
- Young women's beauty is mentioned more than older women's beauty.

Table 13.1: Average Number of References to Physical Appearance and Beauty/Handsomeness by Character's Gender and Age for All Books

All Tales (N = 168)	N	SD
Women's appearance	7.56	14.31
Men's appearance	6.00	7.10
Women's beauty	1.25	2.53
Men's handsomeness	0.21	0.56
Younger women's beauty	1.17	2.11
Older women's beauty	0.08	0.65
Younger men's handsomeness	0.20	0.55
Older men's handsomeness	0.02	0.11

UGLY/BAD, PRETTY/GOOD

At a very young age, children are made to believe that there is a correlation between beauty and goodness and that the heroine of a fairy tale could only be a pretty girl. Similarly, ugliness is associated with evil, e.g., in *Cinderella*, Cinderella's sisters are ugly and evil. In *Sweetheart Roland*, we come across this categorization in a direct manner. 'There was once a woman who was a witch, and she had two daughters, one ugly and wicked, one pretty and good' (Grimm and Grimm, 2000: 187).

In *The Three Little Men in the Wood*, the mother was jealous of her stepdaughter who was 'pleasant and pretty, and her real daughter was ugly and hateful.' Ugliness in women is considered something unacceptable. In *The Skilful Huntsman*, we come across the consequences of ugliness:

> The wedding was fixed, and the maiden had already arrived; because of her great ugliness, however, she shut herself in her room, and allowed no one to see her. . . . (Grimm and Grimm, 2000: 62)

Ugliness is not only considered a social crime but at times it is stretched to the boundaries of sin. In, *Brother and Sister*, the stepmother's own daughter was 'as ugly as sin, and had only one eye'. (Grimm and Grimm, 2000: 297)

GENDER ATTRIBUTES

Thus, fairy tales show a clear division between males and females in terms of attributes. In *Sharing Joy and Sorrow*, the tailor's wife is 'good, industrious, and pious' (Grimm and Grimm, 2000: 18). In *King Thrushbeard*, the king's daughter is beautiful but 'proud and overbearing' (Grimm and Grimm, 2000: 43). In *Clever Gretel*, the female cook is a liar and a glutton, who would eat while cooking. In *The Maiden without Hands*, 'The miller's daughter was a modest and beautiful maiden, and lived in innocence and obedience to her parents' (Grimm and Grimm, 2000: 206). The attributes of the princess in *The Sleeping Beauty*, are summed up in one sentence, 'She was so lovely, modest, sweet, and kind and clever, that no one who saw her could help loving her' (Grimm and Grimm, 2000: 97).

ANIMAL ASSOCIATIONS

It is important to note that male characters in fairy tales are often associated with animals. We come across animal characters including bears, wolfs, frogs, rabbits, donkeys, and lions, etc. This suggests that male characters possess the attributes of animals in terms of strength, swiftness, and domination, etc.

Female characters are dubbed as weaklings, insecure, emotional, and at times troublesome creatures. In, *The Twelve Brothers*, a red flag of warning is associated with the birth of a daughter:

> If a little son is born I will put out a white flag, and then you may safely venture back again; but if it is a little daughter I will put out a red flag, and then flee away as fast as possible as you can, and the dear God watch over you. (Grimm and Grimm, 2000: 431)

THE PROFESSIONS

It is interesting to note that a vast range of professions are mentioned in stories. These professions include tailor, cook, farmer, shoemaker, robber, huntsman, locksmith, musician, surgeon, butcher, woodcutter, carpenter, forester, cook, turner, joiner, miller, baker, apprentice, fisherman, and drummer. Importantly, all the professions in tales belong to the male characters in the stories. Women usually do not figure in professions. However, there are some indoor professions that have been associated with women. There are references to spinning wheels and broom making (*The Elves*), and basket making (*King Thrushbeard*). There is also mention of female characters who are sorceresses and enchantresses. We come across a woman who by profession is a cook, but her character is painted in a negative light. Similarly, another woman can be seen as a beggar by profession.

In the tale, *Fair Katringle and Pif-Paf-Poltrie*, there is an interesting paragraph that not only mentions some of the professions of that time but also their relative significance.

> 'Pif-paf-poltrie, what is thy trade? Art thou a tailor?' 'Something better.' 'A shoemaker?' 'Something better.' 'A joiner?' 'Something better.' ' A smith?' 'Something better.' ' A miller? 'Something better.' 'Perhaps a broom-maker?' 'Yes, that's what I am, is it not a fine trade?' (Grimm and Grimm, 2000: 38)

ASSIGNED ROLES

As a part of the process of socialization, roles are assigned and naturalized by the society. Women are usually confined to domestic chores. Men, on the other hand, move in the public domain, where they are in possession of economic resources to fund domestic expenses. It is interesting to note that, in *Hansel and Gretel*, the witch treats the brother and sister according to their gender.

> Then she grasped Hansel with her withered hand, and led him into a little stable, and shut him up behind a grating; and call and scream as he might, it was no good. Then she went back to Gretel and shook her, crying, 'Get up, lazy bones; fetch water, and cook something nice for your brother. . . .' (Grimm and Grimm, 2000: 105)

In *Old Rinkrank*, the princess ends up in a house where her role is automatically decided.

> The princess had to cook his dinner, make his bed, and do all his work, and when he came home again he always brought with him a heap of gold and silver. (Grimm and Grimm, 2000: 99)

The arrangements are immediately sorted out, as the old man suggests, 'Here you shall have shelter and food; go to the fire, and cook us our supper.'

Similarly in *Snow White*, one of the dwarves shares with Snow White, the tasks that are expected of her.

> If you will keep our house for us, and cook, and wash, and make the beds, and sew and knit, and keep everything tidy and clean, you may stay with us, and you shall lack nothing. (Grimm and Grimm, 2000: 332)

In *Mother Hulda*, a little girl is granted the permission to live in the house, provided she does the assigned chores. She is told this in clear terms. 'Come and live with me, and if you do the housework well and orderly, things shall go well with you' (Grimm and Grimm, 2000: 216). Zipes, quoted in Baker-Sperry and Grauerholz (2003: 714), suggests that:

> Fairy tales written during the eighteenth and nineteenth centuries were intended to teach girls and young women how to become domesticated, respectable, and attractive to a marriage partner and to teach boys and girls appropriate gendered values and attitudes.

FEMALE TORMENTORS

In most of the fairy tales, the tormentors happen to be females, e.g., *Goose Girl*, *The Foundling Bird*, and *One Eye*, *Two Eyes*, *and Three Eyes*, we see a number of stepmothers who are presented as evil characters (*Cinderella*, *Brother and Sister*, *Mother Hulda*, *The True Bride*, *The Lambkin and the Little Fish*, *The Juniper Tree*, *The Three Little Men in the Wood*, and *Hansel and Gretel*, etc.). We also see witches who are architects of evil designs (*Rapunzel*, *Mother Hulda*). In *The Twelve Brothers*, *and Donkey Cabbage*s, we come across a wicked mother-in-law. Fairy tales present some female characters as evil and disloyal, e.g., in *The Little Farmer*, *Old Hildebrand*, and

The Three-Snake Leaves. Therefore, at an early age students get the message that women are the greatest enemies of other women.

Another representation of women is in the form of witches, who are odious in looks and evil in character, e.g., *Hansel and Gretel.* Similarly, wives in fairy tales, in general, are boring, vacuous and timid, e.g., the wife of the giant in *Jack and the Beanstalk*, is frightened of her husband who is the giant.

Unequal Relationship

The gender relationship shown in fairy tales is unequal. Male characters appear to be strong, dominant, generous, and helpful whereas female characters are portrayed as weak, meek, and helpless. The following lines from *Donkey Cabbages*, reflect the unequal relationship:

> The beautiful girl fell on her knees before him, and said, 'Ah, my beloved, forgive me for the evil I have done you; my mother drove me to it; it was done against my will, for I love you dearly'. (Grimm and Grimm, 2000: 256)

Woman: As an Object

In some cases it is declared by the male characters as a challenge to identify and marry a certain girl, as in *The Gifts of Little Folk*, the tailor claims that, 'I shall be master, and marry my dear object (for so he called his sweetheart)' (Grimm & Grimm, 2000: 155). It is important to note the use of the word 'object' for a living being.

Here is an excerpt from the conversation between a hedgehog husband and his wife. The husband wants to run a race with a hare. When his wife asks, 'What can make you want to run a race with the hare?' The husband becomes furious:

'Hold your tongue woman,' said the hedgehog, 'that is my affair. Don't begin to discuss things which are matters for men. Be off, dress, and come with me.' What could the hedgehog's wife do? She was forced to obey him, whether she liked it or not. (Grimm and Grimm, 200: 112)

The husband believes that he has the right to do whatever he likes and is not supposed to 'discuss' matters with his wife. This shows a typical mindset encouraged and conditioned by the patriarchal society.

SACRIFICES OF MOTHERS AND SISTERS

The female character and the notion of sacrifice go together. We see mothers and sisters sacrificing their desires and needs for their kin. In *The Goose Girl*, we see such a mother, whose daughter is about to leave on a journey.

So, when the hour of parting had come, the aged mother went into her bed-room, took a small knife and cut her finger with it until it bled, then she held a white handkerchief to it into which she let three drops of blood fall, gave it to her daughter and said, 'Dear child, preserve this carefully; it will be of service to you on your way'. (Grimm and Grimm, 2000: 66)

In *The Shroud*, we see a typical lonely mother struggling in life patiently.

Then the mother gave her sorrow into God's keeping, and bore it quietly and patiently, and the child came no more, but slept in its little bed beneath the earth. (Grimm and Grimm, 2000: 373)

VOICELESS FEMALES

In some fairy tales, the female characters lose their voice or are forbidden to speak for a certain period of time. This voicelessness of female characters has a symbolic significance, suggesting their lack of voice in patriarchal societies. A similar girl is found in *Our Lady's Child*, 'Although she could not speak, she was so beautiful and charming. . .' (Grimm and Grimm, 2000: 387)

In *The Six Swans*, the sister wishes to rescue her brothers. She can do that on one condition, by losing her voice.

> For six whole years you would be obliged never to speak or laugh, and make during that time six little shirts out of aster flowers. If you were to let fall a single word before the work was ended, all would be of no good. (Grimm and Grimm, 2000: 426)

A similar condition is applied to the sister in *The Twelve Brothers*, who is striving to get her brothers released.

> . . . thou canst not release them but by being dumb for seven years: thou must neither speak nor laugh; and wert thou to speak one single word, and it wanted but one hour of the seven years, all would be in vain, and thy brothers would perish because of that one word. (Grimm and Grimm, 2000: 434)

The condition for female characters to become 'voiceless' in order to survive could be the wishful thinking of a patriarchal society.

DOWRY

When we read fairy tales, we are constantly reminded of the problems faced by women in real life. One of these problems is the curse of dowry. Dowry is a popular practice in South Asia when, at the time of marriage, girls are given gifts by her parents for the new home. The parents make all efforts to make their daughter live comfortably after the marriage. The worst part of it is that the wish list of dowry items is frequently given by the in-laws of the girl. They often become so demanding that marriage cannot take place. In *Fair Katrinelje and Pif-Paf-Poltrie*, a central question is, 'Fair Katrinelje, how much dowry hast thou?' (p. 38). In *The Goose Girl*:

. . . the aged Queen packed up for her many costly vessels and silver and gold, and trinkets also of gold and silver, and cups and jewels; in short, everything which appertained to a royal dowry, for she loved her child with all her heart. (Grimm and Grimm, 2000: 65–66)

DESIRE FOR A CHILD

A recurring theme in some fairy tales is that a king or prominent person has apparently got everything but does not have a child. A number of fairy tales begin thus. *Hans the Hedgehog*, begins with a similar situation:

There once was a country man who had money and land in plenty, but no matter how rich he was, one thing was still wanting to complete his happiness—he had no children. Often when he went into the town with the other peasants they mocked him and asked why he had no children. (Grimm and Grimm, 2000: 484)

One can realize the social pressure but the ultimate stress comes on the wife, who is considered responsible for not having a child, preferably male. In another tale, *The Donkey*, we can feel the agony of a childless wife:

Once upon a time, there lived a King and a Queen, who were rich, and had everything they wanted except one thing: they had no children. The Queen lamented over this day and night, and said, 'I am like a field in which nothing grows.' (Grimm and Grimm, 2000: 481)

CONCEPT OF THE HEROINE

Most of the beautiful good girls in fairy tales suffer from poverty or magic spells or some other predicament, e.g., *Cinderella*, *Sleeping Beauty*, *Rapunzel*, *Snow White*. An early impression about a normal female character children find in the fairy tales is that of helplessness. At times, this weakness is associated with fragile physical structure, as Grandma in *Little Red Riding Hood*, but at other times the weakness is associated with simplicity and naivety, e.g., the character of Little Red Riding Hood.

There are certain gender stereotypes which are perpetuated in fairy tales, e.g., in *Goldilocks and the Three Bears*, the daddy bear's chair and bed are *too high*, and mummy bear's chair and bed are *too soft*. Similarly daddy bear's voice is *gruff* and mummy bear's voice is *sweet*. These stereotypes are based on the taken-for-granted knowledge categorizing human beings on the basis of sex.

Male Saviours

The saviours in most fairy tales are male characters who are physically strong, good natured, helpful and clever. In *Sleeping Beauty*, a prince comes and breaks the magic. In *The Golden Goose*, a boy named Billy helps the princess who forgot to smile. In *Cinderella*, a prince rescues Cinderella from the maltreatment of her stepmother and marries her. In *Snow White and the Seven Dwarfs*, the saviour is also a prince. In *Jack and the Beanstalk*, the male character Jack kills the giant and emerges as a saviour. In *Red Riding Hood*, the male woodcutter comes and saves the girl and her grandmother. In *Old Hildebrand*, the frog prince comes as a saviour. In *The Foundling Bird*, the saviour is a young prince. Similarly, in *Jorinda and Joringel*, the saviour is a male.

In most of these cases, the saviour takes the girl as a trophy and marries her. This happens in a number of fairy tales, including *The Skilful Huntsman*, *Cinderella*, *The Glass Coffin*, *Rapunzel*, and *Sleeping Beauty*.

Waiting for Deliverance

The females are presented as naïve characters, whose only objective in life is to wait for a deliverer and marry him. In *The Three Little Men in the Wood*, the little men with magical powers try to reward a good girl by granting her three things:

. . . the first one said, 'She shall grow prettier every day.' The second said, 'Each time she speaks a piece of gold shall fall from her mouth.' The third said, 'A king shall come and take her for his wife'. (Grimm and Grimm, 2000: 287)

Look at the short speech of the female character in the *Glass Coffin*, who catches sight of the prince and spontaneously utters the following words:

My long-desired deliverer, kind heaven has guided you to me, and put an end to my sorrows. On the self-same day when they end, shall your happiness begin. You are the husband chosen for me by Heaven, and you shall pass your life in unbroken joy, loved by me, and rich to the overflowing in every earthly possession. (Grimm and Grimm, 200: 91)

A similar situation can be seen in *The Water of Life*, where the arrival of the male deliverer is painted like this:

So his horse rode onwards up the middle of it, and when he came to the door, it was opened and the Princess received him with joy, and said he was her deliverer, and lord of the kingdom, and their wedding was celebrated with great rejoicing. (Grimm and Grimm, 2000: 166)

WOMEN WITH MATERIAL NEEDS

Female characters are viewed as creatures with material needs only. In *One-Eye, Two-Eyes, and Three Eyes*, we can see how eating, drinking, and clothing are considered as the ultimate objectives of young girl's life:

So the knight lifted Two-eyes on to his horse, and took her home with him to his father's castle, and there he gave her beautiful clothes, and meat and drink to her heart's content, and as he loved her so much he married her, and the wedding was solemnized with great rejoicing. (Grimm and Grimm, 2000: 182)

IMPOSED MARRIAGES

The female characters are painted as weaklings whose marriages are usually forced by their fathers who often happen to be kings. Examples are *The Frog Prince*, *King Thrushbeard*, *The Robber Bridegroom*, *The Skilful Huntsman*. In a number of cases, the king throws a challenge and offers his daughter as a prize. In *Old Rinkrank*, the king '. . . caused a glass mountain to be made, and said that whosoever could cross the other side of it without falling should have his daughter to wife' (Grimm & Grimm, 2000: 99).

In *The Golden Goose*, there was a king who had a daughter who was so serious that no one could make her laugh. Therefore, '. . . the King had given out that whoever should make her laugh should have her in marriage' (Grimm & Grimm, 2000: 243).

In *The Donkey*, the king becomes concerned about the ailment of his donkey and says:

> 'If I did but know what would make thee content. Wilt thou have my pretty daughter to wife?' 'Ah, yes,' said the ass, 'I should indeed like her,' and all at once he became quite merry and full of happiness, for that was exactly what he was wishing for.' (Grimm & Grimm, 2000: 483)

RARE RESISTANCE

In most cases, the daughters passively follow the orders. But sometimes unjust decrees are challenged. Challenging the king's order is a crime and like any other crime it does not go unpunished. In *The Skilful Huntsman*, an unjust decision is challenged, followed by the pronounced punishment.

> Now as it happened that he had a captain, who was one eyed and a hideous man, and he said that he had done it. Then the old King said that as he had accomplished this, he should marry his daughter. But the maiden said, 'Rather than marry him, dear father, I will go away into the world as far as my legs can carry me.' The king said that, if she

would not marry the captain, she should take off her royal garments and wear peasant's clothing, and go forth, and that she should go to a potter, and begin a trade in earthen vessels. (Grimm and Grimm, 2000: 73)

SEXIST LANGUAGE

Besides the biased content and perspective, the use of language is also sexist. Frequently, the masculine pronoun (he/his) is used for both the genders. In *The Jew among Thorns*, '. . . If I ask a favour of any one *he* shall not be able to refuse it' (Grimm and Grimm, 2000: 40). In *Jorinda and Joringel*, 'If anyone came within one hundred paces of the castle, *he* was obliged to stand still' (Grimm and Grimm, 2000: 276). The explanation that is given for using the masculine pronoun is that it is also generic and does cover the feminine gender. This explanation suggests that women are taken for granted as a subsidiary product.

POLITICS OF LABELLING

It is interesting to note that most of these fairy tales were written by male writers, whose worldview was influenced by patriarchal thinking. The fairy tales, in an interesting manner, reflected the politics of labelling and categorization where roles, expectations, and opportunities for males and females were decided on the basis of sex. The ideal girls/women in stories are supposed to be pretty, tall, fair in complexion, shy, meek, submissive, and compliant. These good females are tormented in the stories by other female characters, e.g., witches, stepmothers, and mothers-in-law who are greedy, vicious, sadistic, callous, and cruel. The good male characters in fairy tales are supposed to be brave, good-natured, cooperative, and smart. Generally, they appear as charming princes who, after saving the girls in plight, marry them. Thus, fairy tales, together with, other social institutions, contribute strongly in the process of manufacturing and perpetuating gendered stereotypes.

PART 5

LANGUAGE, GENDER, AND THE MEDIA

Chapter 14
Gender and Media

> Given the pervasiveness and influence of media in our daily lives, the informal public pedagogies of popular (news and entertainment) media may be surpassing the formal public pedagogies of schooling and postsecondary education in terms of where and how we form citizens.
> — Stack & Kelly

> . . . what is conveyed to us through the mass media is infused with particular values and norms, including many about gender. In other words, the media serve as gender socializers.
> — Renzetti and Curran

Information and entertainment media, which include a number of devices and outcomes, e.g., newspapers, magazines, radio, TV, internet, film, plays etc., in the past few decades has emerged as the most powerful of social institutions and has the capability of influencing minds effectively. It affects societal thought patterns in a subtle manner. According to Diamantopoulou (2000: para 21), 'We cannot underestimate the power of modern, mass media to shape the mentality, attitudes and behaviour of the whole of our society. A balance between men and women at all levels of the media industry is, therefore, vital.

MEDIA: A DOUBLE EDGED SWORD

This important role has positive as well as negative potential, as Anastasio et al. (1999: 155) put it, 'The media, which disseminates information and creates social norms, most likely has the power to build bridges as well as destroy them.'

A popular notion about media is that it reflects what happens in society. In other words, media is considered as a tool of transmission, suggesting that films, plays and newspapers passively mirror the trends of society. This view, however, underestimates the significant role of media as transmission is just one function of the media, the other two very important functions are the construction of social reality and its perpetuation. Renzetti and Curran (2002: 144), referring to the construction function of media, observe, '. . . far from just passively reflecting culture, the media actively shape and create culture.'

MEDIA AND REPRESENTATION

Media acts as a potent tool of representation that can communicate biased perspectives in such a subtle way that the audience imbibes the messages even without knowing it at a conscious level. Anastaiso et al., (1999: 155) suggesting the powerful impact on thought processing observe, 'Not only does the media bias people's perceptions by offering an unrepresentative view of the world at times, but it may also facilitate biased processing of accurate information by presenting that information with an emphasis on inter group differences.'

Media like, other social institutions, take active part in construction of gender in films, TV plays, internet, newspapers, and magazines, etc. This media-mediated representation is usually biased against women. According to Renzetti and Curran (2002: 146):

> A quick perusal of just about any news daily gives one the impression that it is surely a man's world. News of women-centred activities and events, or of particular women (with the exception of female heads of state, women who have died or been killed, and women notable for their association with famous men) is usually reported as *soft* news and relegated to a secondary, 'non-news' section of the paper.

MEDIA REPRESENTATION IN SOUTH ASIA

In the South Asian context, women are underrepresented and misrepresented in the media, according to the findings of the Global Media Monitoring Project (GMMP) 2010. Reporting the findings on differential treatment of women and men, Mohr and Macharia observe (2010: 5), 'Women and men in news stories are often treated differently, displaying significant gender bias. This was found by looking at identification of news subjects by age and family status, and portrayal of news subjects as 'victims' or as 'survivors'.' The GMMP projects, which were conducted after every five years, from 1995 to 2010 show a wide gap in the representation of men and women on television, radio, and newspapers globally. This difference over the years can be seen in Table 14.1:

Table 14.1: Representation of Men and Women in Media

News subjects	1995		2000		2005		2010	
	Women (%)	Men (%)	Women (%)	Men (%)	Women (%)	Men (%)	Women (%)	Men (%)
All media	17	83	18	82	21	79	24	76
Television	21	79	22	78	22	78	24	76
Radio	15	85	13	87	17	83	22	78
Newspapers	16	84	17	83	21	79	24	76
Source: *Global Media Monitoring Project (GMMP) Report 2011*								

MEDIA AND AWARENESS

The media, which plays an important part in creating awareness about gender issues, is simply not working very actively on this front, at least in South Asian countries. In GMMP reports in the South Asian countries, Bangladesh, India, and Pakistan, the percentage of stories involving gender issues which do not highlight gender inequality ranges from 87 to 98 per cent, whereas the percentage of highlighting the issue concerning inequality in these countries ranges from 1 to 4 per cent. This can be seen in the following table:

Table 14.2: Highlighting Issues Concerning Gender in Media

Stories that highlight gender equality or inequality		Does not highlight issues concerning inequality		Clearly highlights issues concerning inequality		Do not know, cannot decide		Total
Region	Country	N	%	N	%	N	%	N
Asia	Bangladesh	295	97	3	1	6	2	304
	India	374	87	25	6	29	7	428
	Nepal	185	98	4	2	0	0	189
	Pakistan	78	95	3	4	1	1	82
Source: *Global Media Monitoring Project (GMMP) Report 2011*								

MEDIA AND RESISTANCE

Media has great potential to resist the onslaught of stereotypes. Unfortunately, the media in South Asian countries is not engaged in challenging gendered stereotypes. Table 14.3, reporting the finding of GMMP report, shows that the media is in fact engaged in reinforcing gendered stereotypes.

Table 14.3: Reinforcing or Challenging Stereotypes

Stories that clearly challenge or reinforce stereotypes		Reinforces stereotypes		Challenges Stereotypes		Neither challenges nor reinforces stereotypes		Total
Region	Country	N	%	N	%	N	%	N
Asia	Bangladesh	49	16	3	1	247	83	299
	India	261	63	37	9	117	28	415
	Nepal	3	2	1	1	183	98	187
	Pakistan	73	90	4	5	4	5	81
Source: *Global Media Monitoring Project (GMMP) Report 2011*								

The invisibility of women in different forms of media suggests deliberate exclusion of the female perspective from this powerful social institution. In South Asian newspapers, especially non-English newspapers, women are represented with a negative bias using provocative adjectives. Rumours and hearsay, together with seductive visuals, are published to attract readers.

POLITICS OF REPRESENTATION

At times, the news may be factual but it is presented with such a linguistic twist that it constructs a negative image of women. In a study conducted by Uks, an NGO in Pakistan (2002), one question was 'Impact of derogatory language in newspapers on women's status and development'. The findings are given in the following table:

Table 14.4: Media Effects on Women

City	Harmful (%)	Harmless (%)
Karachi	60	40
Lahore	91	9
Islamabad	96	4
Peshawar	88	12
Quetta	96	4
Source: *Changing Images*, Uks Report 2004		

In all major cities of Pakistan, it was found that the impact of derogatory language on women was harmful. This harmful impact is relatively greater in Urdu newspapers as compared with English-language newspapers.

WOMEN IN THE MEDIA

An important observation is that relatively few women are working in the media as compared to men. Only a very small percentage of women employees occupy decision-making positions. According to Byerly & Ross (2006: 77):

> The tiny proportion of women working in senior positions in the media, including in film, satellite, and even in the new media, makes clear that the problem is not 'just' with news media, but also with the media industry more generally.

Is this exclusion by coincidence or by design? Tuchman, quoted in Gauntlett (2002: 44), considers it as symbolic annihilation of women by the mass media. Tuchman suggests that from children's shows to commercials to prime-time adventures and situation comedies, television proclaims that women don't count for much. They are underrepresented in television's fictional life—they are 'symbolically annihilated.'

Going beyond Stereotypes

Can journalism afford a balanced portrayal of gender? Mohr and Macharia (2010: 7) suggest, 'News mirrors the world more accurately when the representation of women and men is balanced. Good journalism includes fair gender portrayal.' The Beijing Declaration and Platform for Action (1995, column 6,) rightly suggests,

> Everywhere the potential exists for the media to make a far greater contribution to the advancement of women . . . the continued projection of negative and degrading images of women . . . must be changed. . . . Women must be empowered by enhancing their skills, knowledge and access to information technology.

It is certainly not the case that media can only sell itself at the expense of women, either by excluding them or by exploiting them through biased presentation. It is quite possible to maintain a balanced stance and represent woman on media without biases.

Chapter 15
Women in Advertisements

Advertisements sell the means of production of the look, sealing it in with the mark of feminine desirability, attainable by means of lipsticks, bras, scents and so on—magic formulae, depending on novelty for appeal, just as the market depends on turnover for profit.

– Laura Mulvey

Women are generally subservient to men in ads, both in size and position. Women are often shown as playful clowns, perpetuating the attitude that women are childish and cannot be taken seriously, whereas men are generally portrayed as secure, powerful, and serious.

– Jean Kilbourne

Language and visuals, which used to be considered innocent, neutral, and passive tools of reflection and communication, are now being viewed and studied from totally different perspectives. A number of linguists and social theorists (Hymes, Fairclough, Bourdieu) have advocated that language and visuals are highly political in nature and are not neutral in their essence. They are used as potent tools to construct a certain kind of social reality and perpetuate stereotypes based on a contrived social reality. These also include the stereotypes related to gender.

CULTURE INDUSTRY

A society determines the roles, attaches expectations, and offers opportunities differently for boys and girls. Stereotypes, based on gender construct, are strengthened by repeated use and legitimization by social institutions. These stereotypes are constructed, validated, popularized, and perpetuated with the help of language and visuals through different forms of expression. Advertisements, an interesting form of expression, construct and perpetuate a peculiar kind of corporate logic. This logic provides a recipe for *good citizenship* or conformity with the dominant culture.

GENDERED ADVERTISEMENTS

Advertisements, being persuasive and pervasive in nature, act as potentially powerful *texts* that impact people of all ages. This chapter focuses on advertisements which, through constructing and perpetuating gendered stereotypes, widen the gender gaps and represent women in a biased way. In modern times, advertisements act as a powerful social institution in the process of socialization, which lead to internalization of gendered notions.

GENDERED ADVERTISEMENTS

Some gender-biased stereotypes suggest that women are talkative, less intelligent, cowardly, and confused. These stereotypes, like many others, have no scientific basis. According to Diamantopoulou (2002: para 12), 'Advertising, in particular, continues to promote stereotypical, inaccurate, negative and often degrading images of women, in order to sell products and services.' Nevertheless they are perpetuated through advertisements in an apparently playful but effective manner. For instance, one mobile phone company has a separate package for women with the title, *Ladies First*. The advertisement for this package reads: 'Get beauty tips, cooking recipes, entertainment, shopping, and discounted call rates'. In this short ad, a number of stereotypes are validated and perpetuated.

Some ads try to create humour at the expense of women on the basis of certain stereotypes. In a candy ad, a woman has returned from shopping and is talking non-stop, with the voice-over saying, '*chalti jae, chalti jae, chalti jae*' (it goes on, and on, and on) suggesting the longevity of the candy but there is also a subtle reference to the talkative nature of women.

MARKED ADVERTISEMENTS

The ad for 'Slim' cigarettes suggests that slimness is linked with female attractiveness. The most sensational advertisements are in the domain of make-up products and garments. These focus on products to beautify eyes, lashes, lips, etc. One caption for an ad for lipstick, where a provocative picture is zoomed into, is 'Kiss of approval'. Wykes and Gunter (2005: 43) claim that:

> The first half of the twentieth century certainly saw a re-inscribing of women's bodies. Through advertising they were told clearly that they were women, what women should be, and what that particular product could do to help. Women were both given an identity and told they were not good enough *naturally* at one stroke. However, help was at hand *culturally* as just the right *commodity* to transform them was available for their *consumption*. Women were asked to buy themselves.

EXPECTATIONS FROM WOMEN

As already mentioned, society, in the process of construction of gender, attaches expectations to males and females in a discriminatory manner. Some of the expectations with regard to women in South Asia are that they should always be young, pretty, fair (in complexion), tall and slim.

Expecting every woman to possess these attributes and remain young is unrealistic. There is a whole industry of beauty products that is making a lot of money with provocative advertisements by exploiting the so-called social expectations from women.

Commenting on the cosmetics advertisements, Wykes and Gunter (2005: 48) suggest:

Cosmetic advertising straddles twin discourses of science and beauty whereby the beauty is the goal and the science the means of achieving it. With treatment cosmetics, the authority of science lends credence not just to the efficacy of the product but the legitimacy of the beauty that is the product's goal.

STAY SLIM AND YOUNG ADS

Slimming Centre ads usually print two kinds of pictures: a fat woman before treatment and one less fat woman after treatment at the slimming centre. Again, the stereotype working underneath is that women need to be slim. One would hardly see picture of a man in an ad of for a slimming centre. According to Wykes and Gunter (2005: 13), '. . . during the past few years the problem of young girls systematically starving themselves to death has become a growing area of medical, psychological and finally political concern.' The ad of one beauty cream reads like this: 'Fairness cream for 30+'. The cream is called 'Fair and Ageless'. This expectation from women puts tremendous pressure on them to use such products and fight against the aging process.

WOMAN: AN OBJECT OF DISPLAY

The advertisements of certain products portray women as an object of display where a women is usually seen sitting on an elevated platform. In a particular one ad for shoes, a woman is shown posing with a shoe. This ad suggests the presentation of woman as a commodity. Mulvey (2009: 22), referring to the display of women suggests, 'Thus the woman as icon, displayed for the gaze and enjoyment of men, the active controllers of the look, always threatens to evoke the anxiety it originally signified.' Peach (2008: 211) suggests that, '. . . studies on the projection of women in Indian advertisements in the past have shown that women were mostly projected as glamorous or enticing, whether they were used to sell cosmetics, fabrics, jewellery, domestic appliances, suitcases, scooters or stationery.'

MESSAGE AROUND WOMEN BODIES

In one of the advertisements for a local airline, the names of different cities are written on the body of a woman. The caption reads: 'The most relaxing way to fly'. In an ad for ice cream, the caption that goes with the woman's picture is ' All indulgence' In an ad for garments, a women is wrapped up with neckties and the caption reads, 'I am all tied up with. . . .' Kuntjara (2001: 98) sums up the image of an ideal woman portrayed in the advertisements:

> Conventional beauty is her only attribute. She has no lines of wrinkles, is young, no scars, pores or blemishes. She is thin, generally tall and long-legged. All 'beautiful' women in ads conform to this norm. Women are constantly exhorted to achieve this ideal, to feel ashamed and guilty if they fail, and to feel that their desirability and lovability are contingent upon physical perfection.

PROVOCATIVE IMAGES

In some cases, the actual product for which the ad is made is hardly seen. What is more noticeable is the provocative picture of a woman. Even in certain ads which have no relevance to women, we still see them for 'aesthetic' purposes. For instance, shaving foam or razor blade ads where a man is shaving while a women stands and watches him with interest. Commenting on such ads, Rukh (1996: 70) writes:

> While the machismo male image is perpetuated, the women stand behind the male models, not even in active supportive roles but simply applauding male successes. Masculine strength, power and expertise is glamorized and idealized in contrast to the passive, backstage role given to women.

THE FEMININE TOUCH

In a number of products, one sees the magical 'feminine touch' which is the creation of the innovative minds of ad designers. For instance, in ads for mattresses, a woman would either be lying on it or stroking the surface with her hand. Similarly, in a motorbike ad, a woman caresses the seat with her hand.

The most unfortunate part of these ads is that the models, used are provided the best conditions in the studios with a lot of makeup, but act as role models for ordinary women.

As discussed before, such ads create unrealistic expectations and women take tremendous pressure on them to look like the models shown in the ads. Mulvey (2009: 56) comments on this social pressure by suggesting that:

> The female body has become industrialized; a woman must buy the means to paint on (make up) and sculpt (underwear/clothes) a look of femininity, a look which is the guarantee of *visibility* in a sexist society for each individual woman.

THE MAGIC OF BEAUTY CREAM

Some ads for 'fairness' creams for lightening the complexion show a girl who is hopeless about her marriage prospects suddenly finding the magic cream that makes her complexion fair. This discovery is followed by the jubilant wedding music. Orbach, cited in Wykes and Gunter (2005: 72), reflects on the potential impact of such ads on an ordinary woman:

> She attempts to make herself in the image of womanhood presented by billboards, newspapers, magazines and television. . . . She is brought up to marry by catching a man with her good looks. To do this she must look appealing, earthly, sensual, virginal, innocent, reliable, caring, mysterious, coquettish and thin.

Such advertisements aim at transforming women. This pressure is enhanced through the female models used in the ads. Gauntlett (2003: 129), referring to Cronin, suggests that, 'Consumerism promises women self-transformation and appears to validate women's choices. Yet, even as subjects, women have faced an impossible imperative 'to be ourselves' through 'doing ourselves' mediated by 'doing' make-up (making yourself up), fashion (fashioning yourself), dieting and exercise (re-forming yourself).' The negative impacts of these ads include anxiety and pressure as Renzetti and Curran (2002: 409) suggest:

> . . . since body image is strongly linked to self-esteem, rigid un-attainable beauty norms cultivate in women and girls anxiety about and dissatisfaction with their appearance, starting at an early age.' (Allgood-Merton et al., 1990; Strauss, 1999; Ussher, 1989; Whitaker et al., 1990)

NEED TO PORTRAY A POSITIVE IMAGE OF WOMEN

Such ads perpetuate gendered stereotypes on a mass scale. Media, being a powerful tool of socialization, validates these stereotypes and manufactures the consent of society at large. Women, in the wake of the media onslaught, internalize these stereotypes as facts. Chomsky (2004b: 27) commenting on the impact of media writes:

> That's all there is in life. You may think in your own head that there's got to be something more in life than this, but since you're watching the tube alone you assume, 'I must be crazy,' because that's all that's going on over there.

There is a serious need to realize how words and images are involved in the constant construction of social reality and we should be using them with a lot of care. There is a need to design ads which are not gendered in nature. Portraying a positive image of women may help us reduce the gender gaps in real life.

Chapter 16
Television Plays and Gender Stereotypes

> In their traditional exhibitionist role women are simultaneously looked at and displayed, with their appearance coded for strong visual and erotic impact so that they can be said to connote to-be-looked-at-ness.
>
> – Laura Mulvey

> . . . many Pakistani women share a special intimacy with television because gender segregation and the division of labour mean they spend most of their time in the confines of domestic space.
>
> – Shuchi Kothari

There used to be a rich tradition of mobile stage theatres in South Asia in the late nineteenth and early twentieth centuries. These theatres, in the absence of modern day cable TVs and films, were a significant source of entertainment. This old tradition of theatres was followed by talking movies, which have made their mark universally. The changing pace of life, however, prompted a number of cinemagoers to look for alternative modes of entertainment. This alternative came in the form of television, which started in India in 1959 and in Pakistan in 1964.

SIGNIFICANCE OF TELEVISION

The popularity of television was due to a number of socio-economic factors. People found a mini-cinema at home, which they could watch at their leisure time. Initially, television programmes were more family driven and all the member of a family could sit, watch and enjoy these programmes. In India, the state owned channel Door Darshan was available to all the viewers. The apparent objectives set by the television programmes were education and entertainment. In Pakistan, television broadcasting started in 1964 with the single state owned channel PTV (Pakistan Television).

TELEVISION PLAYS

The first play that was aired on PTV was *Nazrana*. In 1984, PTV started colour transmissions which made the television programmes more attractive. The first colour TV drama aired on PTV was *Phool Walon Ki Sair*. It was the sole channel and people would wait for the next episode of a play on TV. There were famous playwrights like Shaukat Siddiqui, Ashfaq Ahmed, Amjad Islam Amjad and on the other hand some very popular serials written by female playwrights such as Bano Qudsia, Fatima Surraiya Bajia, Haseena Moin, and Noor-ul-Huda Shah. The popularity of these plays could be attributed to a political factor as well. During General Mohammad Ziaul Haq's military dictatorship, cinema was systematically discouraged and as an alternative television plays were encouraged to provide curtailed entertainment to people confined within their homes. Consequently, many of the most famous television plays were aired on PTV during Zia's regime. The whole emphasis of Zia's policy was a didactic media which could pass on moral values to the viewers.

ATTITUDES TOWARDS GENDER

Ashfaq Ahmed's series of plays *Aik Mohabbat Sau Afsane*, *Tota Kahani*, *Aur Drame*, etc. portrayed a stereotypical image of women, where male characters occupied the central place and female characters were mere objects of love. These plays were interspersed with long dialogues which at times would appear as moral sermons. Interestingly, these plays tried to challenge some stereotypes but, at the same time, perpetuated some other stereotypes, including a conservative image of women.

Amjad Islam Amjad was another writer whose TV serials set new standards of popularity. *Waris* proved to be a trendsetter for TV dramas. It was a popular Pakistani drama that revolved around the corrupt feudal system of the country, depicting landowners as greedy and arrogant, while the peasants were suppressed and victimized. This influence was not only restricted to the rural domain but was extended to the city of Lahore as well. This drama brought social injustice to the forefront and revealed the hidden face of feudalism. All the powerful characters in the play, however, were male.

Amjad's other serials *Sumandar*, *Dehleez*, and *Raat* were very popular. In all these serials, men played dominant roles and women were presented as docile and submissive. In some cases, where women were portrayed as independent, they were set in a negative light. For example, Mrs Maryam Bari, who works for the rights of women, is at times ridiculed and presented as a hypocrite, odds with her husband and daughter. The overall atmosphere of Amjad's serials is andocentric, where women play a secondary role. Commenting on the plays written during the years of General Mohammad Ziaul Haq, Hussain (1996: 25–26) claims that:

> The entire focus is on her reproductive or potentially reproductive and nurturing capacities, and no space is allowed where her economic dimension might be acknowledged. Thus she is denied a separate identity as well as the power to control her own life.

THE FEMALE PLAYWRIGHTS

Besides male playwrights, we see some important female writers as well. Bano Qudsia was prominent playwright but most of her plays took their inspiration from the idea of positional superiority of men. Her perspective on life coincides with that of Ashfaq Ahmed, her husband, who believed in the perpetuation of traditional values. Fatima Surraiya Bajia wrote a number of famous plays, which focused on small issues at family level in an entertaining manner. Bajia was also interested in communicating certain morals through her plays, mostly in line with the status quo. Haseena Moin wrote a number of plays for TV, including *Ankahi*, in which the protagonist is an ambitious girl Sana Murad who belongs to a lower middle class family and yearns for a wealthy life. The drama foregrounds Sana's development as a character from a juvenile girl to a mature individual. What is noteworthy in the drama is the way Haseena Moin instils her leading female character with impetuosity and a vivacious charm that enlivens the lives of those who come in contact with her.

Another of Haseena Moin's serials that gained popularity was *Tanhaiyan*. This is a Pakistani drama that deals with the story of two sisters who lose their parents in a car accident. What seems contentious in this drama is the portrayal of a successful businesswoman as a failure in terms of her relationships. Therefore, here the trope of a woman who has escaped from the premises of home attaches negative connotations with itself. Yet, from another perspective the drama also suggests that in a patriarchal society a woman has to sacrifice her affective sensibility to be at par with men.

DRAMAS WITH A DIFFERENCE

Noor-ul-Huda Shah made a real contribution by writing plays which were radical in their content, as they tried to challenge some taboo themes by locating women in the cruel patriarchal system of feudalism. Her plays like *Deewar*, *Jungle*, and *Asman Tak Deewar* were a great source of education and awareness of women's identity in a strong patriarchal system and brought forth issues of gender in an upfront manner. Asghar Nadeem Syed's, *Pyaas* was another important play that dealt with a tabooed theme. Shahid Nadeem who worked in PTV as a producer and later on as general manager wrote some memorable plays that focused on women's issues with bold treatment. Thus, a number of hitherto taboo themes related to women were brought to light through the genre of drama.

DRAMA TURNS COMMERCIAL

During the last decade, TV drama *has* undergone a tremendous change. This change can be seen both in India and Pakistan. One major reason in both the cases is the introduction of private channels that mainly started as business ventures. In India, during the early 1990s, private channels started their programmes. In Pakistan a number of private TV channels were given licences in the late 1990s. These private channels were essentially linked with commercialism and started showing dramas which were quite different from the ones aired previously. A major change was that drama was brought closer to film and thus became more glamorous and louder. Large budgets were allocated for the production of dramas which would also attract commercials. Since the number of channels increased, the frequency of TV plays also increased. A direct consequence of enhanced frequency was new scriptwriters, new directors, and new actors and actresses. The increased demand of dramas by a number of channels resulted in the lowering of quality. A number of serials of Indian TV channels are watched in other countries including Pakistan. Some of these serials include *Kyonki Saas Bhi Kabhi Bahu Thi*, *Biddai*, *Kahani Ghar Ghar Ki*, and *Kasauti Zindagi Ki*.

Kyonki Saas Bhi Kabhi Bahu Thi is a drama that shows the evolution of three generations in one household. It revolves around the powerful industrialist Virani family and reveals the strife that weakens it from within. The conspiratorial figures are the elder daughters-in-law of the family and their victim is Tulsi, daughter of a poor family and wife to Mihir the eldest grandson. The intrigue to dismantle Tulsi's marriage is the driving force behind this soap. The drama, while presenting Tulsi as a strong woman with the ability to weather all storms, at the same time perpetuates the stereotype of women as tricksters playing family politics.

Bidaai is an Indian drama, a story of two cousins, Sadhna and Ragini. Sadhna is the orphaned cousin, and is pretty looking. Ragini, the elder, lacks beauty. While, on one hand, Sadhna finds her position in the family a little precarious due to her beauty, Ragini has to suffer the censure of society for being unpresentable as a prospective daughter-in-law. The drama plays with the binaries of ugly/pretty and fair/dark yet fails to dismantle the split, because it again seeks salvation for the unpresentable Ragini in the image of a handsome man. As a result, beauty still stands high in the hierarchy of appearances.

Kahani Ghar Ghar Ki, is an Indian soap that tells the story of a family, involving a manipulating mother-in-law, devious sister-in-law and several daughters-in-law, who struggle to claim a place in the hierarchy of a family unit. The drama constructs a good/evil divide through the conflict the self-sacrificing Parvati, the eldest daughter-in-law of the Agarwal family, and malevolent Pallavi the younger daughter-in-law of the family. Jealousy, hatred, suspense, and family politics are central themes of this drama. This depiction of women fails to capture their dynamism and instead constructs them in shades of black and white which affects the perception of the society at large.

Kasauti Zindagi Ki, was another Indian soap that revolved around the classic love story of Anurag and Prerna, two star-crossed lovers who suffer through numerous trials and tribulations yet are destined to remain apart. The class conflict here appears to be in direct relation to the gender conflict. Men belonging to the wealthier classes make decisions of love and strife while women either use devious means to hinder their plans or sacrifice themselves to support them.

PRESENTATION OF AN UNREALISTIC WORLD

These serials are very popular among women. They are essentially melodramatic in nature and far removed from the realities of life. The mansions and bungalows shown in the dramas are unreal. Women are always clad in glamorous dresses and made up for display. A typical theme in these dramas is unending conflict between *Saas* (mother-in-law) and *Bahu* (daughter-in-law). The representation of women in these dramas is biased. Women are shown as conspiratorial, back-biting and hypocritical. These television dramas are watched by millions of people in South Asian countries on a daily basis. A large part of the audience is women. They project stereotypical gendered views that become part of the audience through the process of internalization.

CONTEMPORARY WOMAN IN TELEVISION

The Centre for Advocacy and Research (2003: 1685) maintains that

> The serials deal with issues women come across in their everyday life. While these serials do raise controversies (due to the stereotypes they reinforce), they also allow women from different strata and walks of life to identify with the same issues. The identification is not just at the level of consciousness but also at the material level.

Television plays, being very popular among the masses, especially among females, act as one the most potent sources of constructing and perpetuating gendered messages, false expectations by society, and unattainable dreams. They mount psychological pressures on young females to be like the perfect female character presented in the plays, living in posh mansions and having all the worldly facilities. Thus, the ultimate potential outcome is frustration and depression. There is a serious need to revisit television plays in terms of their plots, diction, setting, characters and messages.

Chapter 17
Construction of Gender in Films

Most slang terms for women in her corpus are negative, and most deal with physical appearance and sexual promiscuity; by contrast, far fewer terms for men are negative, and those that are do not have the same focus upon the body and sexuality.

— Hall and Bucholtz

A central feature of the imperialist structure is that the interaction is asymmetrical. This can be clearly seen in media imperialism, one of the branches of cultural imperialism which has been extensively researched, and which has affinities with linguistic imperialism in education system.

— Robert Phillipson

Films and theatre are supposed to recreate real life situations and simulate social life on screen and stage. A popular tradition of theatre was strengthened by the Urdu Parsee theatre. According to famous script writer and lyricist Javed Akhtar, quoted in Kabir (2003: 50) 'The early Urdu Parsee theatre first produced adaptations of Shakespearean and Victorian plays, and these plays were presented in a certain style: they had drama, comedy and included many songs.'

MOTION PICTURES

We then see a phase of silent movies, where life was emulated in the form of motion pictures. A revolution in performing arts, however, came when the talking movies took over and with the passage of time India became a centre of film making. Now every year in India hundreds of movies are produced, which are shown on thousands of cinemas to millions of people in and outside India. According to Kabir (2003: v) ' In India, with the proliferation of satellite and cable channels, Hindi cinema's power and influence have become even greater as we enter the new millennium.' A large population in India, Pakistan, and other countries, watches these movies on CDs, DVDs, and internet. In Pakistan, the film industry is not very active but theatre is catching on, especially in big cities like Karachi and Lahore.

PORTRAYAL OF WOMEN

The popularity of film and theatre in the subcontinent suggests the vital role they play in the construction of social realities, such as gender. One reason of this popularity could be our oracy-based society. According to Javed Akhtar, the famous Indian lyricist (Kabir, 2003: 57), 'Our cinema is still heavily influenced by traditional theatre, and so cinema heavily relies on the spoken word.'

A number of gender-related stereotypes are constructed, popularized, advocated, legitimized and perpetuated by films and theatre and, since they are very popular media, their impact is rapid and wide. In the movies of the 1960s in the subcontinent, we see a submissive prototype of women whose docility is her virtue. On the other hand, men are presented as strong, brave, and patronizing. Women are shown as weak, helpless, and thus dependent on men. According to Lee (2008: 11) '. . . female protagonists are generally portrayed as weak, passive, and victimized, so they are incapable of independent action or of living an authentic life. . . .'

ACTIVE ROLE OF WOMEN

The so called active role for women can be found in 'dances' where women are portrayed as sex symbols. Sher (1996: 43) explores the rationale of such provocative scenes in films, '. . . because patriarchal cultures designate the woman as 'object of desire', the eroticism of such cinema projects the woman as the legitimate object of male desire and fantasy.'

Indian films are distinguishable from Western films in terms of the numbers of dances and songs. The dances, in most cases, have nothing to do with the story line or situation. They are there as a commercial need as it is believed that the main attraction for the masses is provocative dances, executed by women in scant clothing. Eckert and McConnell-Ginet (2003: 34) suggest: 'The gender order is a system of allocation, based on sex-class assignment, of rights and obligations, freedoms and constraints, limits and possibilities, power and subordination. It is supported by—and supports—structures of *convention*, *ideology*, *emotion*, and *desire*.'

THE INEVITABLE RAIN

Another ingredient to enhance the desired impact of a dance is the inevitable rain in which the heroine dances. Thus, women are objects of display. Mulvey (2009: 17) observes:

> Freud isolated scopophilia as one of the component instincts of sexuality which exist as drives quite independently of the erotogenic zones. At this point, he associated scopophilia with taking other people as objects, subjecting them to a controlling and curious gaze.

In a number of film scenes, women dance to entertain male characters. The dances have become such an integral part of films that huge funds are invested for sets and costumes of the dancers. According to Gopalan (2002: 37), 'A more daring technique foregrounds the female body through extreme close ups of waist, breasts, and hips. A masterful employment of this technique is seen in Ramesh Sippy's *Sholay/Flames* (1975).' All this is done in order to satisfy the *gaze* of spectators.

LANGUAGE IN FILM AND THEATRE

The heroines are inevitably women out of this world. They are not ordinary women but near to perfection as far as the physical appearance is concerned. At least four ex-Miss World titleholders are acting in Indian films. These actresses are slim and are made stunningly beautiful with the help of make-up and studio lights. The girls who watch such stars attempt to look like them.

CHANGE IN LANGUAGE

The choice and use of words in movies went under a tremendous change over the last five decades. In the early 1950s and 1960s, we see the use of formal language, which was literary in nature. This Hindi/Urdu language used in movies was highly Persianized. The female characters behaved strictly according to the prevalent cultural norms. The heroines in the movies were required to speak in soft, low tones, with a touch of coyness. The language, however, became simpler and more direct with the passage of time. The flavour of Persian diminished and English words became common in dialogues. If we look at the titles of some contemporary Indian Hindi movies, we see a blend of English and Hindi words, e.g., *Singh is King*, *Jab We Met* (When We Met) or *U, Me, aur Hum* (You, Me, and Us). The image of the heroine changed from a coy woman to an outgoing girl. But in both of these roles, exploitation of a different kind was in action. The heroines of contemporary Urdu/Hindi films are *Phoolan Devi*, *Miss Hong Kong*, *Miss Colombo*, and *Jano Kapatti*, etc.

LANGUAGE OF FILM AND THEATRE

Some of the songs employ double meanings and manifest obscenity. This is very common in the stage plays where dialogues cross the limits of decency. The female characters are often presented as foolish and are made the butt of jokes. The language of theatre plays is usually so obscene that a family sitting together cannot watch such plays.

Most of the stereotypes about women, e.g., women are weak, cowardly, dependent, emotional, stupid, capricious, talkative, etc., are perpetuated and promoted by both film and theatre. Similarly some positive stereotypes about men, for instance, that men are strong, brave, independent, stable, and clever, etc., are advocated in these movies. All this is done in such a playful and make-believe manner that the audience perceive it as reality. A large number of people who watch these movies in cinema or on CDs,/DVDs and internet are influenced by them.

WAY AHEAD

Who is responsible for the misrepresentation of women in films and theatre? The list may include film financers, film directors, story writers, dialogue writers, and song writers. The majority of them are men who try to represent women with their own biases and desires. Consequently, it is not an honest representation. Some female directors tried to bring about change but others opted to move with the tide.

SOME POSITIVE INITIATIVES

Some notable Indian films that highlighted the gender issue include *Lajja*, *Kalki*, *Provoked*, *Silent Waters*, *Matrubhoomi*, *Monsoon Wedding*, *Kya Kehna*, *Shakti* etc. *Lajja* by Raj Kumar Santoshi is a story of female subjugation. It is a story of four women and how they have been subjected to heinous treatment by men in various stages of life. *Matrubhoomi: A Nation without Women*, by Manish Jha is based on sexual aggression, where a group of barbaric, sex-starved men marry one woman and rape her night after night by turn. *Provoked* by Jagmohan, casting Aishwarya Rai Bachchan is based on the subject of domestic violence. It is the true story of a woman from Punjab who married a man in England. *Kya Kehna*, directed by Kundan Shah and starring Preity Zinta is another movie based on the struggle of a woman who has a child out of wedlock and finally wins respect for herself. Krishna Wamsi's film *Shakti*, starring Karishma Kapoor, focuses on the mother–son relationship. This is a story of a mother who would go to any limit for the love of her son.

NEED OF A CRITICAL MASS

Is it possible to bring change in terms of themes, language use, and representation of women? The answer is a definite yes, but for that a more creative approach is required. We do find some good movies that touched on social issues without using the crutches of songs and dances and misrepresentation of women. For this change, we need a critical mass of educated, talented, and creative people. We also need more women coming to the fields of script writing, song writing, and direction. It is high time that films and media are used to challenge some of the taboos of society instead of strengthening and perpetuating them.

Chapter 18
Representation of Women in Songs

They've left us only lacks, deficiencies, to designate ourselves. They've left us their negative(s).

– Luce Irigary

. . . rationality is a very narrowly restricted skill. Only a small number of people have it. Most people are guided by just emotion and impulse. Those of us who have rationality have to create 'necessary illusions' and emotionally potent 'oversimplifications' to keep the naïve simpletons more or less on course.

– Noam Chomsky

South Asian oracy-based societies have a robust tradition of poetry and singing. Most of our folk poetry, e.g., Baba Farid, Shah Latif Bhitai, Bulleh Shah, Khushhal Khan Khattak, Mian Muhammad, Shah Hussain, and Kabir, is still recited with musical tunes. The popularity of poetry in India and Pakistan has several reasons. For one, it is easy to memorize a verse as compared to a piece of prose. Also, poetry has the capability of touching emotions and heightening the impact of a message. This impact is further enhanced when poetry is recited. We see a strong tradition of *mushairas* in the Indian subcontinent, where poets would recite their poetry and people in large number would listen to them and appreciate their poetry. The role of songs in movies in the subcontinent is pivotal and no film is considered complete without songs.

SONGS AND HEGEMONY

The popularity of songs in the oracy-based societies of India and Pakistan make them a potent source of influencing the masses. This apparently playful source of entertainment is an important tool of hegemony. Songs have the capability of constructing, popularizing, perpetuating, and legitimizing certain stereotypes, helping in hegemonizing the marginalised groups. Being a tool of social construction, they play an important part in the construction and perpetuation of gender stereotypes. The songs used in films are linked with women in different ways. Most of these songs, in term of their content, deal with women. A number of songs in films are accompanied by dances by female characters. Also, most of the songs are sung by women. In this way, songs contribute in manufacturing the image of women.

BINARY DIVISION IN SOCIETY

Let us look at the lyrics of some of the songs in order to understand the process of construction, perpetuation, and validation of gender related stereotypes. Before we actually analyse the lyrics, it is important to understand the dynamics of the male and female divide. The division of male/female can be understood in relation to the binary system at work in our society. This system talks about day and night, strong and weak, and high and low, etc. The problem begins when one is considered good and other as bad, e.g., good/bad, normal/abnormal, standard/deviant, and natural/weird, etc. Robinson (2004: 45) suggests that:

> The fundamental contribution of cultural studies has been to illustrate the ways in which cultural hegemony is perpetuated in representations of popular culture. Music is not a transcendent, natural, or universal art form, but rather a social construction shaped by structural forces, dominant ideologies, the conventions of technology, and the hegemonic values of white, Western patriarchy.

POWER AND JUSTIFICATION

This kind of labelling has its own politics where certain groups in society are permanently dubbed as weak and others as 'standard'. The politics of categorization always favours the powerful. Let us look at the lyrics of the song 'Dholan' sung by Hadiqa Kiani, a Pakistani singer. The song is in Seraiki, where a girl is singing and addressing her beloved. The girl compares herself with a *maid* and calls her male lover as a *King*. She considers her own 'real pearls' as false and the 'fake coins' of her beloved as precious as silver. This song shows that power plays its role in justifying certain things and condemning the others. A related aspect is the Gramscian notion of 'spontaneous consent', where the marginalised group is conditioned to believe that their own culture, identity, language, and heritage are inferior as compared to those of dominant groups as the girl in the song believes that all her possessions are worthless—even her real pearls are adjudged by her as false.

DESCRIBING BY PHYSICAL FEATURES

The politics of representation shows that, where men are described with reference to their achievements, women are described in terms of their physical features. This process of representation perpetuates certain kinds of stereotypes regarding roles and expectations. Some of the expectations include that a woman should be beautiful, young, tall, slim, and fair. For instance, in a song in the Indian film, *1942—A Love Story*, the hero of the movie describes the physical beauty of the heroine, using all kinds of similes. Let us look at some of comparisons used to admire the physical beauty of the heroine:

> When I saw that girl
> She appeared to me
> Like a blossoming rose
> Like a poet's dream

Like a bright ray of light
Like a deer in woods
Like a moonlit night
Like a musical discourse
Like a lamp lit in a temple
Like beauty of morning
Like sunshine in winter
Like a flute's tune
Like the essence of colours
Like a winding vine
Like playing waves
Like fragrance borne on a cool breeze
Like a dancing peacock
Like a silky string
Like fairies' song
Like sandalwood fire
Like perfect embellishment
Like light drizzle
Like gradually growing intoxication

In another Indian movie, *Welcome*, there is a song, '*Ek Uncha Lamba Qad*' (Tall in Height) that celebrates the height of the female beloved. A very popular song, sung by the Pakistani band Vital Signs is '*Gore Rang ka Zamana*' (The Age of Fair Complexion).

Gore rang ka zamana kabhi ho ga na purana	The age of fair colour will always be in vogue
Gori dar tujhe kis ka hai	What scares you then, O *Gori*? (fair-coloured woman)
Tera to rang gora hai	As you have a fair complexion
Sanwla salona rang kis ko bhata hai	Nobody goes for darkish complexion
Jise dekho gorion ke peeche chala aata hai	Everybody follows women of fair colour

The song highlights the benefits of a fair complexion for girls and suggests that the preference of society for a fair complexion will never end. The interesting line of the song is where the singer assures the girl that she need not worry about anything, because she has a fair complexion.

This exaggerated depiction of physical beauty is common in Indo–Pak film songs. Here is a song from an Indian film *Badshah* (The King).

Kahin zulf ka badal o ho,	Somewhere it is a cloud of long hair
Kahin rangili anchal aa haa,	Somewhere it is a colourful veil
Kahin hont gulabi o ho,	Somewhere it is pink lips
Kahin chaal sharabi aa haa,	Somewhere it is intoxicated gait
Kahin jism ki khushboo aa haa,	Somewhere it is the fragrance of the body
Kahin narma nigahen o ho,	Somewhere it is soft looks
Kahin gori bahen aa haa.	Somewhere it is white arms

Besides fair complexion, a slim figure, especially a slender waist, is another desired feminine attribute. The following song from a Bollywood movie *Aashiq*, reflects these desirable attributes and perpetuates a fair complexion and slim figure.

Gore gore gaal mere baheki baheki chaal hai	My cheeks are white and my gait is swinging
Dekh meri patli si kamariya har aashiq behaal hai	Every lover becomes frenzied after seeing my slender waist

The film songs are not just confined to the description of physical appearance but, at times, they also perpetuate behavioural stereotypes, e.g., tentativeness attributed to women. This song from the movie, *Chori Chori*, alludes to this gendered stereotype.

Main sochoon haan kar doon, dil bole na kar de	I think of saying 'yes', but my heart says 'no'
Dil bole haan kar de, main sochoon na kar de	My heart suggests I say 'yes', but I think I will say 'no'
Haan, main sochoon haan kar doon, dil bole na kar de	I think I will say 'yes', but my heart says 'no'
Dil bole haan kar de, main sochoon na kar de	My heart suggests I say 'yes', but I think I will say 'no'

OBJECTIFICATION OF WOMEN

A number of songs present woman as an object that can be displayed and appreciated on the basis of its external features and use. Sheppard, quoted in Robinson (2004: 46), suggests that:

> . . . as reflections of the male desire to control the world, women themselves must be controlled and manipulated. This is accomplished by means of their isolation and objectification. The conceptualization of people as objects decontextualized from social relations implies the possibility for uncontested, unilateral control.

The politics of representation is much deeper as dominant groups paint the marginalised groups with their biases. Some famous song writers in India and Pakistan include Sahir Ludhianvi, Jan Nisar Akhtar, Gulzar, Javed Akhtar, Tanveer Naqvi, Ahmed Rahi, and Riaz ur Rehman Saghar. All these songwriters are male. They represent women from their own perspectives. The ironic aspect of the whole situation is that the biased representation of women by the songwriters in the form of lyrics is executed by female singers through singing and acting.

FROM DIVERSITY TO ONENESS

Male behaviour is promoted as *standard* and is thus considered
natural. Any deviation from it is looked down upon. It is interesting
to note the insistence of dominant groups that other sub groups
should act according to the standards set by the dominant groups.
A song in the Indian movie *Hum Tum* (Me and You), is '*larki kyun
na jaane kyun larko si nahin hoti?*' (Why is a girl not like a boy?).
This apparently innocent question reflects the deeply embedded
desire of the dominant group to make others come to the melting
pot in order to become one with the dominant group. The *Hum
Tum* song also makes use of certain stereotypes for instance 'girls
think a lot but understand less'. Here are a couple of lines from a
Hindi song with their translation:

Larki kyon na jaane kyon ladko si nahin hoti	Why is a girl not like a boy?
Sochti hai zyada	She thinks a lot
Kam woh samajh thi hai	But understands little
Dil kuch kehta hai	Her heart says one thing
Kuch aur hi karti hai	But she does the other

In the stereotyped gendered expression, we see some welcome
experiments by certain lyricists. For instance, the following lines of
a song from the Indian film *U, Me aur Hum* talk about maintaining
the identities of lover and beloved:

Apne Rang Ganwae Bin, Mere Rang Mein Ghul Jaao	Without losing your colour, dissolve into my colour
Apni Dhoop Bujhaye Bin, Meri Chhaon Mein Aa Jao	Without extinguishing your sunshine, come to my shade
O Chalo Yun Kare,	O Let us do this
Tum, Tum Bhi Raho, Main, Main Bhi Rahoon	You remain you, and I, remain I
Hum, Hum Bhi Rahein	Us remain Us

Tum, Tum Bhi Raho, Main, Main Bhi Rahoon	
Hum, Hum Bhi Rahein	
Teeno Mil Ke Saath Chale	The three of us move forward together
Saathi Janam Janam, U Me Aur Hum.	O my friend
U Me Aur Hum, U Me Aur Hum.	You, me and us.

PICTURIZATION OF SONGS

Besides the lyrics of songs, their actual picturization is also biased and presents women as objects of display. For instance, a typical scene in Indian and Pakistani movies is that the heroine keeps on dancing to please the hero, who stands in a corner unconcerned. Gopalan (2002: 37) commenting on the nature of commercial films songs suggest:

> A classic and familiar montage in romantic song and dance sequence offers an overview of the landscape while the camera zooms in on the actors. In cutting between close-ups of the lovers and a panoramic vision of a lush landscape, the alternating segment introduces us to a possible kiss before cutting away.

This situation needs to be changed. The change can be initiated at different levels, i.e. family, educational institution, judiciary, media, etc. There is a serious need to challenge the gender related stereotypes. Language used in songs helps in constructing, perpetuating, and legitimizing these stereotypes. The songwriters need to take a fresh look at the situation and instead of following age-old analogies and images, try to construct new idioms and images which are non-sexist in nature.

PART 6

GENDERED DISCOURSE: REFORM AND RESISTANCE

Chapter 19
Need for Language Reform

. . . twentieth century European feminism has been constitutionally torn between fighting against over feminization and against under-feminization, especially where social policies are concerned.

– Denis Riley

At stake is a power structure in which certain people, often without being conscious of it, just assume the right to tell other people who they are.

– Deborah Cameron

In the past, the whole focus of language and gender research was to look at the language differences between men and women. In recent times, the focus of language and gender research has shifted from language spoken *by* women to language spoken *about* women. This shift raises questions about the politics of representations constructed largely with the help of language. Spender's book, *Man Made Language*, offers the interesting thesis that, like other cultural forms, men controlled language and, as a result, one can see more positive words for males with a lot more opportunities to use them. Since language is a powerful tool to construct social reality, the dominant group, with the help of language use, represents woman as an inferior deviant. The perpetuation of this negative representation of women takes place in diverse situations through multiple modes. According to Goddard and Patterson (2000: 31), '. . . in describing men and women physically, men tend to have "physiques" while women have "figures". The connotations of these two terms are very different: physique suggests physical strength and body size, while figure connotes aesthetic shapeliness and sexual attractiveness.'

Validation by Social Institutions

The process of validation in social institutions further 'confirms' the inferior female status to the extent that a large number of women start viewing themselves in a negative light. Can identities be changed? What role can language play in the process of constructing identities?

Rationale of Language Reforms

If language is a vital force in constructing, validating, and perpetuating the differences, can language reforms play a role in reducing the gender gap? One group of linguists, researchers, and practitioners endorse this idea. They believe that it is important to get rid of gendered expressions and create new words, terms, and expression which are not biased against any gender. According to them, there are two simple reasons for avoiding the use of gendered language.

First, that as we use the gendered language we in fact own it and validate its gendered messages. According to Goddard and Patterson (2000: 57), 'Stereotyping is very much about the process of applying a simplified model to a real, complex individual, often to negative and derogatory effect.'

Second, that the more we use these gendered expressions, the more we engage ourselves in strengthening these messages. According to Austin (1962), we *do* things by using language. This suggests that language itself is involved in performing things, in this case gender. This concept is further strengthened by Butler (*Gender Trouble*) in 1990, where she suggests that repetitive expressions construct gendered bodies. The more we use gendered language, we realize that sexist impressions turn into what is 'natural' and 'common sense' and become a part of the psyche of the given society. There have been gender biases in connotation, collocations and generic use of expression. Renzetti and Curran (2002: 139) cite example of these categories in Table 19.1.

Table 19.1: Sexism and Language

Connotations	Generic He/Man
governor-governess	policeman
master-mistress	spokesman
patron-matron	manpower
sir-madam	social man
bachelor-spinster	mankind
Word Pairs	workman's compensation
brothers and sisters	'Man the oars!'
husband and wife	he, him, his
boys and girls	

INITIATIVES IN LANGUAGE REFORM

There have been some efforts to reforms the language. For instance, where the title 'Mr', used for men whether they are married or unmarried, the suggested title for women is 'Ms', irrespective of their marital status. This, to some extent, addresses the problem of mandatory revelation of marital status through the use of the titles 'Miss' or 'Mrs'.

In case of using the generic masculine pronoun for both men and women, the problem can be avoided by writing s/he. This can also be tackled by using the plural expression (they, their, them) instead.

Discriminatory job titles were revised by US department of labour [cited by Goddard and Patterson (2000: 74)]. These alternatives were an attempt to combat ageism and sexism:

Table 19.2: Alternative Expression

Original Term	New Term
airline steward, stewardess	flight attendant
foreman	supervisor
salesman	salesperson
seamstress	sewer
signalman	signaller
watchman	guard
draftsman	drafter
junior executive	executive trainee
camera man	camera operator
office girl, boy	office helper
repairman	repairer
fireman	firefighter
spokesman	spokesperson
policeman	police officer
chairman	chairperson, chair
housewife	house manager

Sunderland (2006: 12) lists some alternative expressions to replace the gendered and marked expressions:

Table 19.3: Alternative Expression

Alternative item	Intended to replace	Reason
Ms	*Miss/Mrs*	to achieve equivalence with *Mr* and to end the practice of women being 'defined' by their marital status
chairperson *spokesperson* *barperson*	*chairman* *spokesman* *barman* (especially as referents for women)	to put an end to the 'think male' phenomenon, and the 'rendering invisible' of women
s/he, 'singular *they*'	'generic *he*'	as above
doctor *usher* *flight attendant*	*lady doctor* *usherette* *air hostess*	to achieve equivalence with 'masculine' terms, and to end the practice of 'trivializing' and 'marking' feminine terms

This language reforms agenda, however, should not be confined to surface level changes; it should also tap the deep level intentions of the expression. For instance, we need to revisit the sayings and proverbs which are so commonly used in daily life situations as 'logical evidence' from the repertoire of folk wisdom. A number of these sayings and proverbs are biased against women. Similarly, jokes about women are also based on gendered stereotypes. Likewise, in a number of Hindi/Urdu songs women are defined only in terms of their physical beauty and are presented as objects of display. There is a need to challenge these gendered stereotypes through our social institutions, such as families, educational institutions, judiciary, media, etc. Such sayings, jokes, and songs need to be discouraged at all levels. According to Renzetti and Curran (2002: 141), 'Given that women are denigrated, unequally defined, and often ignored by the English language, it serves not only to reflect their secondary status relative to men in our society, but also to reinforce it. Changing sexist language, then, is one of the most basic steps we can take toward increasing awareness of sexism and working to eliminate it.'

THE CONSERVATIVE STANCE

The conservative school of thought, however, has a contemptuous view of language reforms and dismisses any such initiative. Some self-concocted examples of language reform are presented for the purpose of ridicule. For instance, Manchester where 'man' needs to be replaced as it is 'sexist.' Such absurd examples are deliberately created to dismiss the very idea of language reform by the anti-reform group. This mindset is tied up with status quo forces that discourage any change.

THE RADICAL VIEWPOINT

The radical approach of feminists has its own reservations about language reforms. These reservations have a different rationale as feminists hold that language reforms at vocabulary level are of not much use as the problem is much deeper. According to the radical school of thought, the whole language system is androcentric and bringing change in just some expressions is of little use. Cameron, quoted in Ehrlich, S. & King, R. (1994: 60) makes a similar point:

> . . . in the interests of accuracy we should strive to include the female half of the human race by replacing male terms with neutral ones. But the 'reality' to which language relates is a sexist one, and in it there are no neutral terms. . . . In the mouths of sexists, language can always be sexist.

MEANINGS AND SOCIETY: A DIALECTIC RELATION

One school of thought believes that gender differences in real society should be reduced. Once gender equality is achieved, the linguistic gender biases would be automatically taken care of.

This viewpoint appears convincing but the underlying assumption is that language is a passive phenomenon which is not involved in action. Language, on the contrary is a highly political phenomenon. Far from being a passive and neutral tool of communication, it is actively involved in the construction of social reality. Spender (1998: 31), rightly suggests that:

> As more meanings are changed so will society change and the sexist semantic rule be weakened; as the society and the sexist semantic rule changes so will more meanings change-without deliberate intervention. To concentrate on either word meanings or social organizations—to the exclusion of the other—is to invite failure.

A more holistic approach is to avoid the either/or distinction and work on both fronts, i.e. social equality in real society and linguistic equality through language reforms at the same time.

Chapter 20
Resistance through Language

> . . . language is the primary means through which we maintain or contest old meanings, and construct or resist new ones.
>
> – Eckert and McConnell-Ginet

> . . . it is unrealistic to expect radical change. Change can take place in the society, however. An essential step in creating that change is understanding and challenging the cultural myths and stereotypes. Above all, as always, we must break the silence.
>
> – Jean Kilbourne

Language plays an active part in the construction of social reality. The vital linkage between knowledge and discourse has been elaborated by Foucault in his works *Archaeology of Knowledge* (1972), and *Discipline and Punish* (1995). According to him, *knowledge* and *power* strengthen and justify each other as constructed discourses which lead to a certain kind of knowledge that in turn justifies those discourses. The dominant groups in a society make use of language to construct desired social realities that favour them by ensuring their superiority in an apparently 'objective' manner. According to Atanga (2010: 40) 'Power also consists of occupancy of positions, which carry with them the power of command over others. Such occupancy is accompanied by specific language use and this language is the language of power.' Fairclough's book *Language and Power* (2001) also underscores the central role of language in the politics of representation and construction of social reality.

Language and Social Institutions

In all social institutions, the role of language is central in the process of socialization and in the acquisition of social knowledge. For instance, the language used in media strongly impacts the perception of readers/viewers. According to Renzetti and Curran (2002: 145), 'There is considerable evidence indicating that many media consumers, particularly heavy television viewers, tend to uncritically accept media content as fact.' In all imperialistic initiatives, language has been exploited as a powerful and effective tool for hegemonic purposes. The language of the dominant groups possesses certain perks and to enjoy those perks the marginalised groups have to act according to the linguistic and cultural rules of the dominant groups. It is important to note that access to language is strategically made conditional by the dominant groups.

Can marginalised groups challenge the hegemony of dominant groups? How can marginalised groups be empowered to identify the politics of representation? Is resistance through language possible? What changes are required in the existing practices of English Language Teaching? These are some major questions taken up in this chapter.

Foucault is of the opinion that power is in fact a relationship which is largely structured by discourse. According to Foucault, the powerful and powerless keep on changing during different points in history as this relationship is not fixed. This also means that points of resistance are available to the marginalised groups to tilt the balance of power in their favour. There seems to be a constant struggle for the possession of discourse in order to possess or regain power. Balliger, cited in Robinson (2004: 47), explains this dynamic: 'Hegemony, while saturating all arenas, is, however, never complete because oppositional practices affect and shape the hegemonic process.'

RESISTANCE TO HEGEMONY

Similarly, female identity does not have a fixed status. With changing times, it may also change. Khan et al. (1994: 2) suggest that:

> In a fragmented world, identities are also fragmented, multilayered, conflicted and, therefore, basically open. Identity is a dynamic process, an on going negotiation of the self with the world. It is perpetually created and recreated. It is in a constant state of becoming.

Tilly, cited in Lukes (2005: 10), tries to explore the possible answers to the question of why subordinate groups do not put up resistance to the dominant groups all along?

1. The premise is incorrect: subordinates are actually rebelling continuously, but in covert ways.
2. Subordinates actually get something in return for their subordination, something that is sufficient to make them acquiesce most of the time.
3. Through the pursuit of ends such as other-valued esteem or identity, subordinates become implicated in systems that exploit or oppress them. (In some versions, no. 3 becomes identical to no. 2).
4. As a result of mystification, repression, or the sheer unavailability of alternative ideological frames, subordinates remain unaware of their true interests.
5. Force and inertia hold subordinates in place.
6. Resistance and rebellion are costly; most subordinates lack the necessary means.
7. All of the above.

REVERSING THE DISCOURSE

As we see in the list, resistance to hegemony can happen in different ways. Some of them may not be very effective. For instance, in the

Indo-Pak subcontinent, a group of people, mostly conservative Muslim clerics, refused to learn English as it was the language of the colonisers. This response to English cost them dearly in terms of jobs, social status, etc. Another response to hegemony, which seems to be more effective, could be to learn the language and resist through it, by reversing the discourse, as Foucault would call it. This approach requires us to familiarize ourselves with the discourses of the powerful and discern the allied aspects of power in those structures. This identification is not possible if language is viewed and learnt only as a neutral and passive phenomenon. There is a direct implication for studying applied linguistics.

REDEFINING APPLIED LINGUISTICS

Pennycook (2001) underlines the importance of studying language with its socio-political aspects, dealing with the questions of representation, politics, and power. It is this critical study which empowers the learners to see the political use of language and the power structures constructed with the help of language. Fairclough (1989) proposes this empowerment through critical discourse analysis where learners are sensitized to see the power in the text and behind the text. The awareness of political use of language may help the learners towards the next step of actually negotiating meaning and using discourse for putting up resistance.

REVISITING ELT PRACTICES

Schools, like other social institutions, play an important part in conveying and legitimizing stereotypes. According to Canagarajah (1999: 28):

> The school shapes the consciousness and behaviour of the students by distributing the cultural practices of the dominant groups as the norm. Students who acquired this linguistic and cultural capital would grow to justify and serve the interests of the dominant groups.

How can this biased view of gender be changed? The good thing about the notion of gender is that, since it is a social construct, it is not fixed. The same social agencies that have created a skewed view of women can be geared towards challenging and reforming the existing gendered social structures. In addition to the family, educational institutions and media can play their part in two important ways. As mentioned before, stereotypes get their strength by frequent use and legitimization through certain social institutions. If our schools and media can help by not perpetuating the fixed gendered notions they would not gain legitimacy. Going one step further, educational institutions and media can challenge these stereotypes and thereby support the process of resistance and reconstruction.

SCHOOLS AND HEGEMONIC STEREOTYPES

In schools and other educational institutions, stereotypes can be promoted as well as challenged. Certain notions, for instance, the notion of gender, where male superiority is considered as something natural, can be challenged in the classrooms. Eckert and McConnell-Ginet (2003: 13) suggest that:

> To whatever extent gender may be related to biology, it does not flow naturally and directly from our bodies. The individual's chromosomes, hormones, genitalia, and secondary sex characteristics do not determine occupation, gait, or use of colour terminology.

ELT SCENARIO IN PAKISTAN

The ELT practices in the India and Pakistan need to be revisited. In mainstream educational institutions, language has been taught as a neutral phenomenon and there has been emphasis on grammatical rules of language. Canagarajah (1999: 20) explores the reason for treating language as a neutral and passive phenomenon:

It suited ELT to define language and teaching as a value-free cognitive activity, since in that way its material and ideological interests in spreading English globally could be conveniently ignored.

There is a need to expose the students to the potent relationship of language and power. The use of critical pedagogy in the teaching of English in our language classrooms can bring a qualitative change in the thinking patterns of students. They can revisit the stereotypical concepts by unpacking them linguistically. There is also a genuine need to make English teaching more interdisciplinary in order to understand some major concepts in a more holistic manner. Canagarajah (1999: 28) suggests that the 'The redefinition of constructs such as subjecthood, culture, power, and knowledge by resistance theories has enabled us to conceptualize the potential for teachers and students to negotiate power.' A critical approach to teaching of language empowers students to challenge the familiar, popular, and taken-for-granted meaning of words and concepts. Derrida's notion of deconstruction is relevant to this discussion, as he focuses on 'delaying the meaning' of words by challenging the fixity of their meanings and connotations.

WOMEN AND LACK OF ACCESS TO LANGUAGE

In South Asian societies, women constitute a large group but the control usually lies with men. If we have a cursory look at the sayings, proverbs, jokes, songs, text books, films, and TV plays in South Asian societies, we see the active hegemony of men. This hegemony is largely wielded through the use of language. Spender (1998) suggests that it is men who are in the position of control, including the language with which they represent women. The gendered stereotypes which constitute the folk wisdom of a society are constructed, perpetuated and legitimized by language. A similar point is emphasised by the American critic Elaine Showalter, quoted by Cameron (1990: 10):

The appropriate task for feminist criticism is to concentrate on women's access to language . . . on the ideological and cultural determinants of expression [i.e. the social rather than the psychic]. The problem is not that language is insufficient to express women's consciousness but that women have been denied the full resources of language and have been forced into silence, euphemism and circumlocution.

HOLISTIC APPROACH TO RESISTANCE

The resistance to hegemony needs a more holistic approach towards language teaching, language learning, and language use. Educational institutions can play an important role by making sure that gendered stereotypes are not validated by teachers in the classrooms. Equally important is the point that the language should be taught with a critical approach, so that students should be able to challenge some of the stereotypes which are based on 'common sense' and 'taken for granted.' According to Wallowitz (2004: 26):

The critical reader understands that *how* we read is as important as *what* we read and asks questions about the construction of a text: Who is the assumed audience? What is the hidden agenda? How does the text reflect and shape notions of gender? What ideal audience is being created?

WOMEN AND GENDER CONSTRUCTION

Sometimes women themselves are inadvertently involved in perpetuating gendered stereotypes. In the process of resistance, the individual's role and responsibility is very important. One should not expect that change will come automatically. In the process of resistance and change, one needs to be patient, determined, and creative.

MEDIA AND RESISTANCE

The role of media becomes crucial in challenging the gendered stereotypes. According to Renzetti and Curran (2002: 162), '. . . the media, particularly television, can be a powerful force in breaking down sexist stereotypes by sensitively and realistically portraying women and men in nontraditional roles.' The gender inequality problem is so pervasive in South Asian society that just legislation and formal education cannot cope with this challenge. The appropriate use of media should be made to combat the gender inequality challenge as suggested by Diamantopoulou (2002: para 23): 'The media should be used, rather, as a tool to promote a positive and realistic image of women. We must also fill the research gap surrounding women and the media.'

NEED FOR NETWORKING

The act of resistance should not be left to marginalised groups alone but civil society should play its role to encourage and facilitate this process. Similarly, marginalised groups should also reach out for social networking. Chomsky (2004b: 40–41) believes that:

> Organization has its effects. It means that you discover that you're not alone. Others have the same thoughts that you do. You can reinforce your thoughts and learn more about what you think and believe. These are very informal movements, not like membership organizations, just a mood that involves interactions among people.

Can we take a start in our educational institutions to empower the students, through critical pedagogy in ELT, challenge the gendered stereotypes in the shape of sayings, proverbs, jokes, and songs, etc.? The educational institutions need to offer courses focusing on the sociopolitical aspects of language, making students realize how language acts as a powerful tool to construct social realities, including gender. Besides offering such courses, we also need to have a critical pedagogy to inculcate critical thinking and reading skills to enable students to analyse a discourse, written or spoken, to understand hegemonic structures constructed and perpetuated with the help of language. These efforts in schools should be linked and strengthened by other social institutions, especially media. The media, because of its entertaining style, wide range, and fast pace could play a complimentary role with schools to challenge gendered myths and promote equitable representation of people irrespective of their gender.

Bibliography

BOOKS

Afkhami, M. (ed.). (1995). *Faith and Freedom: Women's Human Rights in the Muslim World.* New York: I.B. Tauris & Co. Ltd.

Ahmad, M. (ed.). (2001). *Urdu Zarb-Ul-Amsaal Aur Kahawatain* (Urdu Proverbs and Sayings). Lahore: Ferozsons Private Limited.

Ahmad, R. (ed. & trans.). (1990). *Beyond Belief: Contemporary Feminist Urdu Poetry.* Lahore: ASR Publications.

Arat, Z.F. (ed.). (1999). *Deconstructing Images of 'The Turkish Woman'.* Hampshire: Palgrave Macmillan.

Atanga, L. (2010). *Gendered Discourse in the Cameroon Parliament.* Bamenda, Cameroon: Langaa RPCIG.

Austin, J. (1962). *How to do Things with Words?* Oxford: Oxford University Press.

Aziz, C. (ed.). (2003). *Dawat Lataief.* Lahore: Sang-e-Meel Publications.

Bayoumi, M., and Rubin, A. (eds.). (2001). *The Edward Said Reader.* London: Granta Books.

Berge, B-M., and Ve, H. (2000). *Action Research for Gender Equity.* Buckingham: Open University Press.

Bergvall, V., Bing, J., and Freed, A. (eds.). (1996). *Rethinking Language and Gender Research: Theory and Practice.* London: Longman.

Bhasin, K. (2008). 'Challenges for Women's Empowerment and Education in South Asia: The Goal is Empowerment of Human Values'. In M. Bhatia, D. Bhanot, and N. Samant (eds.). *Gender Concepts in South Asia: Some Perspectives.* Jaipur: Rawat Publications.

Bhatia, M., Deepali, B., and Nirmalya, S. (eds.). (2008). *Gender Concepts in South Asia: Some Perspectives.* Jaipur: Rawat Publications.

Brizendine, L. (2006). *The Female Brain*, London: Bantam Books.

Burke, L., Crowley, T., and Girvin, A. (2000). *The Routledge Language and Cultural Theory Reader.* London: Routledge.

Butler, J. (2000). 'From Parody to Politics'. In Burke, L., Crowley, T., and Girvin, A. *The Routledge Language and Cultural Theory Reader.* London: Routledge.

Butler, J. (1990). *Gender Trouble: Feminism and Subversion of Identity.* New York and London: Routledge.

Butler, J. (1993). *Bodies That Matter: On the Discursive Limits of 'Sex'*. London: Routledge.

Byerly, C., and Ross, K. (2006). *Women & Media: A Critical Introduction*. Oxford, UK: Blackwell Publishing.

Cameron, D. (ed.). (1990). *The Feminist Critique of Language*. London: Routledge.

Cameron, D. (1996). 'The Language-Gender Interface: Challenging Co-option'. In V. Bergvall, J. Bing, and A. Freed. *Rethinking Language and Gender Research*. London: Longman.

Canagarajah, A. (1999). *Resisting Linguistic Imperialism in English Teaching*. New York: Oxford University Press.

Candlin, C. (1989). 'Introduction'. In N. Fairclough. *Language and Power*. London: Longman (1st edition).

Carroll, D. (2008). *Psychology of Language*. Belmont: Thomson Wadsworth.

Chomsky, N. (1992). *Deterring Democracy*. London: Vintage Books.

Chomsky, N. (2004b). *Media and Control*. Lahore: Vanguard.

Chomsky, N., and Otero, C. (2004a). *Language and Politics*. Oakland: AK Press.

Cixous, H. (2000). 'The Laugh of the Medusa'. In Burke, L. Crowley, T. and Girvin, A. *The Routledge Language and Cultural Theory Reader*. London: Routledge.

Coates, J. (2004). *Women, Men, and Language*. Great Britain: Pearson Education Limited.

Cohn, B. (1996). *Colonialism and Its Forms of Knowledge: The British in India*. Princeton: Princeton University Press.

Coltrane, S. (2000). *Gender and Families*. Oxford: AltaMira Press.

Comely, N., and Scholes, R. (1994). *Hemingway's Genders*. Pennsylvania: Yale University Press.

Crawford, M. (1995). *Talking Difference*. London: Sage Publications.

D'Souza, P. (2005). *Woman: Icon of Liberation: A Work-Book for Exploring and Achieving Total Liberation*. Mumbai: Better Yourself Books.

De Beauvoir, S. (1949). *The Second Sex*. Translated by H.M. Parshley (1997). London: Vintage Classics.

Eckert, P., and McConnell-Ginet, S. (2003). *Language and Gender*. Cambridge: Cambridge University Press.

Fairclough, N. (1989). *Language and Power*. London: Longman (1st edition).

Fairclough, N. (2001). *Language and Power*. London: Longman (2nd edition).

Farooqi, S. (2002). '*Taneesiat ki Tafheem*' (Understanding Feminism). In Hussain, K. and Naheed, F.A.K. (eds.). *Intikhab: Khawateen ka Aalmi adab* (*Selection: Women's World Literature*). Islamabad: Academy of Letters.

Feldman, J. (1993). *Gender on the Divide*. Ithaca: Cornell University Press.

Flueckiger, J.B. (1996). *Gender and Genre in the Folklore of Middle India*. New York. Cornell University Press.

Flynn, E., and Shweickart, P. (eds.). (1986). *Gender and Readings*. Maryland: The John Hopkins University Press.

Foucault, M. (1972). The *Archaeology of Knowledge*. London: Tavistock.

Foucault, M. (1978). *The History of Sexuality: An Introduction*. Harmondsworth: Penguin.

Foucault, M. (1980). *Power/Knowledge: Selected Interviews and Other Writings, 1972–1977*. Edited by Colin Gordon. New York: Pantheon Books.

Foucault, M. (1995). (2nd edition). *Discipline and Punish: The Birth of the Prison*. Translated by A. Sheridan. New York: Vintage.

Friedman, M., & Narveson, J. (1995). *Political Correctness*. London: Rowman & Littlefield Publishers, Inc.

Gauntlett, D. (2003). *Media, Gender and Identity: An Introduction*. London and New York: Routledge.

Giddens, A. (2006, 5th edition). *Sociology*. Cambridge: Polity Press.

Goddard, A., and Patterson, L. (2000). *Language and Gender*. London: Routledge.

Gopalan, L. (2002). *Cinema of Interruptions*. New Delhi: Oxford University Press.

Gramsci, A. (1996). *Selections from the Prison Notebooks*. Hyderabad: Orient Longman.

Gray, J. (1993). *Men are from Mars, Women are from Venus*. London: Thorsons.

Grimm, J., and Grimm, W. (2000). *Grimm's Fairy Tales*. Michigan: Border Classics; Harmondsworth: Penguin.

Halai, A. (2007). 'Boys are Better Mathematicians! Gender Issues in Mathematics Classrooms in Pakistan'. In Qureshi, R. and Rarieya, J.F. (eds.) *Gender and Education*. Karachi: Oxford University Press.

Hall, K., and Bucholtz, M. (1995). *Gender Articulated*. New York: Routledge.

Hameed, Y. (2007). *Takhleeqi Amal aur urdu shair i nisai tanazur mein* (Creative Process and Urdu Poetry from Women Perspective). *Adabiaat*, Islamabad: Pakistan Academy of Letters.

Harrington, K., Littosseliti, L., Sauntson, H., and Sunderland, J. (2008). *Gender and Language Research Methodologies*. Hampshire: Palgrave Macmillan.

Hasan, F., and Farrukhi, A. (2003). *Khamoshi ki awaz* (Sound of Silence). Karachi: Wada.

Hellinger, M., and Busmann, H. (2002). *Gender across Languages*. Amsterdam: John Benjamin's Publishing Co.

Hussain, N. (1994). 'Women as Objects and Women as Subjects within Fundamentalist Discourse'. In Khan, N., Saigol, R. and Zia, A. *Locating the Self: Perspective on Women and Multiple Identities*. Lahore: ASR Publications.

Hussain, N., Mumtaz, S., and Saigol, R. (eds.) (1997). *Engendering the Nation-State* (Vol. 2). Lahore: Simorgh Women's Resource and Publication Centre.

Hussain, N., Mumtaz, S., and Saigol, R. (eds.) (1997). *Engendering the Nation-State* (Vol. 1). Lahore: Simorgh Women's Resource and Publication Centre.

Hussain, N., Shah, N., Sher, F., & Rukh, L. (1996). *Reinventing Women*. Lahore: Women's Resource and Publication Centre.

Hymes, D. (1972). 'On Communicative Competence'. In Pride, J.B. & Holmes, J. (eds.). *Sociolinguistics*. Harmondsworth, England: Penguin Books.

Ingham, P. (1996).*The Language of Gender and Class: Transformation in the Victorian Novel*. London: Routledge.

Jameel, I. (2002). *Urdu Afsana aur Aurat* (Woman and the Urdu Short Story). In Hussain, K. and Naheed, F.A.K. (eds.). *Intikhab: Khawateen ka Aalmi adab* (Selection: World Women's Literature). Islamabad: Academy of Letters.

Jasam, S. (2001). *Honour, Shame and Resistance*. Lahore: ASR Publications.

Jaworsky, A., and Coupland, N. (eds.). (2006). *The Discourse Reader*. London: Routledge.

Jesperson, O. (1922). *Language: Its Nature, Development and Origin*. New York: Allen and Unwin.

Kabir, N. (2003). *Talking Films: Conversation on Hindi Film with Javed Akhtar*. New Delhi: Oxford University Press.

Khan, A., (1999). *Rhetoric and Reform*. Lahore: ASR Publications.

Khan, N., Saigol, R., and Zia, A. (eds.). (1994). *Locating the Self: Perspective on Women and Multiple Identities*. Lahore: ASR Publications.

Korte, B. (1993). *Body Language in Literature*. Toronto: University of Toronto Press.

Kovecses, Z. (2006). *Language, Mind, and Culture*. New York, OUP.

Lakoff, R. (2004). *Language and Woman's Place*. New York: Oxford University Press.

Longman Group Ltd. (1978). *Longman Dictionary of Contemporary English*. Essex: Longman.

Lukes, S. (2005). *Power: A Radical View*. New York: Palgrave Macmillan.

Macaulay, T.B. (2004). 'Minute'. In Rahman, T. (ed.) *Language and Education*. Islamabad: National Institute of Pakistan Studies, Quaid-e-Azam University.

Mahmud, S. (1988 new edition). *Angare (Burning Coals)*. Sweden: Kitabiat.

Malik, M., and Hussain, N. (1985). *Reinventing Women*. Lahore: Simorgh Women's Resource and Publication Centre.

Maltz, D., and Borker, R. (1982). 'A Cultural Approach to Male-Female Mis-communication'. In John Gumperz (ed.). *Language and Social Identity*. Cambridge: Cambridge University Press.

Mansoor, S., Azam, S., Zafar, M., and Tatari, S. (2007). 'Gender and Language in Higher Education'. In Qureshi, R. and Rarieya, J.F. (eds.). *Gender and Education*. Karachi: Oxford University Press.

Mansoor, S, Meraj, S., and Tahir, A. (2004). *Language Policy Planning and Practice*. Karachi: Oxford University Press.

Mariniello, S. and Bove, P.A. (eds.). (1998). *Gendered Agents*. Durham: Duke University Press.

Millet, K. (1969). *Sexual Politics*. Urbana: University of Illinois Press.

Mohawarat-o-Zarb-ul-Amsaal (Proverbs and Sayings). Lahore: Ferozsons Private Limited.

Mulvey, L. (2009). *Visual and Other Pleasures*. Hampshire: Palgrave Macmillan.

Mumtaz, K., and Shaheed, F. (1987). *Women of Pakistan: Two Steps Forward, One Step Back?* Lahore: Vanguard Books.

Nanda, A.R., and Jagatdeb, L. (2008). 'Girl Child: Socio Demographic Implications for South Asia'. In Bhatia, M. et al., *Gender Concepts in South Asia: Some Perspectives*. New Delhi: Rawat Publications.

Orwell, G. (1989). *Animal Farm*. London: Penguin Books.

Pallegrini, A. and J. (1994). 'Play, Toys and Language'. In Goldstein, J.H. (ed.). *Toys, Play, and Child Development*. New York: Cambridge University Press.

Peach, L. (2008). 'Gender Imagery in American and Indian Advertising: Some Comparative Notes'. In Bhatia, M. et al. (eds.), (2008). *Gender Concepts in South Asia: Some Perspectives*. New Delhi: Rawat Publications.

Pennycook, A. (1994). *The Cultural Politics of English as an International Language*. Harlow: Longman Group Limited.

Pennycook, A. (2001). *Critical Applied Linguistics: A Critical Introduction*. Mahwah: Lawrence Erlbalm Associates, Inc.

Philipson, R. (1992). *Linguistic Imperialism*. Auckland: Oxford University Press.

Qaiser, W. (ed.). (2002a). *Muskarahatein* (Smiles). Lahore: Alfaisal Publishers.

Qaiser, W. (ed.). (2002b). *Shokhiyan* (Cheerfulness). Lahore: Alfaisal Publishers.

Qureshi, R., and Rarieya, J.F. (eds.). (2007). *Gender and Education in Pakistan*. Karachi: OUP.

Rahman, T. (ed.). (2004). *Language and Education*. Islamabad: National Institute of Pakistan Studies, Quaid-e-Azam University.

Rahman, T. (1996). *Language and Politics in Pakistan*. Karachi: Oxford University Press.

Rahman, T. (2002). *Language, Ideology and Power*. Karachi: Oxford University Press.

Rasool, N. (2007). *Global Issues in Language. Education and Development: Perspectives from Postcolonial Countries*. Clevedon: Multilingual Matters Ltd.

Renzetti, C., and Curran, D. (2002). *Women, Men, and Society*. Boston: Pearson Education, Inc.

Riaz, F. (2003). *Khamoshi ki Aawaz* (Sound of Silence). Karachi: Wada Kitab Ghar.

Ricento, T. and Wiley, T. (2004). *Journal of Language and Education*. Special Issue (Re) constructing Gender in a New Voice. New Jersey: Lawrence Erlbaum Associates, Publishers.

Rizvi, H. (2000). *The Military and Politics in Pakistan: 1947–1997*. Lahore: Sang-e-Meel Publications.

Romaine, S. (2000). *Language in Society: An Introduction to Sociolinguistics* (2nd edition). Oxford: Oxford University Press.

Rukh, L. (1996). 'Advertisements'. In Hussain, N.; Shah, N.; Sher, F., Rukh, L., *Reinventing Women*. Lahore: Women's Resource and Publication Centre.

Said, E. (1978). *Orientalism*. New York: Pantheon Books.

Saigol, R. (2000). *Symbolic Violence*. Lahore: SAHE Publications.

Saussure, F. (1960). *Course in General Linguistics*. (ed.). C. Bally and A. Sechehaye in collaboration with A. Reidlinger, trans. W. Baskin. London, Peter Owen (rev. edn. 1974). First published in 1916.

Schultz, M. (1990). 'The Semantic Derogation of Woman'. In Cameron, D. (ed.). *The Feminist Critique of Language*. London: Routledge.

Seidman, S. (2003). *The Social Construction of Sexuality*. New York, Norton & Company, Inc.

Sellers, S. (1994). *Helene Cixous Reader*. London: Routledge.

Shaukat, N.A. (ed.). (2004). *Mischiefs*. Lahore: Aslam Ismat Printing Press.

Shaukat, N.A. (ed.). (2004). *Shokhiyan* (Cheerfulness). Lahore: Aslam Ismat Printing Press.

Siddiqui, S. (2010). *Rethinking Education in Pakistan: Perceptions, Practices, and Possibilities*. Karachi: Paramount Book Publishers.

Singer, J. (1994). 'Imaginative Play and Adaptive Development'. In Goldstein, J.H. (ed.). *Toys, Play, and Child Development*. New York: Cambridge University Press.

Spender, D. (1990). 'Extracts from Man Made Language'. In Cameron, D. (ed.). *The Feminist Critique of Language*. London: Routledge.

Spender, D. (1998). *Man Made Language*. London: Pandora Press.

Sugden, J., and Tomlinson, A. (2002). *Power Games: A Critical Sociology of Sport*. New York: Routledge.

Sultanoff, S. (1995). *What is Humour?* (Electronic version).

Sunderland, J. (2006). *Language and Gender*. New York: Routledge.

Sunderland, J., and Litosseliti, L. (2008). 'Current Research Methodologies in Gender and Language Study'. In Harrington, K., Littosseliti, L., Sauntson, H., and Sunderland, J. (eds.). *Gender and Language Research Methodologies*. Hampshire: Palgrave Macmillan.

Tannen, D. (1992). *You Just Don't Understand! Women and Men in Conversation*. London: Virago.

Thanvi, A. (1997). *Bahishti Zevar* (Heavenly Ornaments). Karachi: Taj Company.

Trudgil, P. (1983 revised edition). *Sociolinguistics: An Introduction to Language and Society*. Middlesex: Penguin.

Uks—A Research, Resource and Publication Centre on Women and Media. (n.d.). *Changing Images: A National Study on Monitoring and Sensitisation of the Print Media the Portrayal of Women*.

Wardhaugh, R. (2006). *An Introduction to Sociolinguistics*. Oxford: Blackwell Publishing.

Warren, V. (2011). Guidelines for Non-sexist Use of Language. American Philosophical Association.

Wegener-Spohring, G. (1994). 'War Toys and Aggressive Play Scenes'. In Goldstein, J.H. (ed.). *Toys, Play, and Child Development*. New York: Cambridge University Press.

Wodak, R. (ed.). (1997). *Gender and Discourse*. London: Sage Publications.

Woolf, V. (1990). 'Women and Fiction'. In Cameron, D. (ed.). *The Feminist Critique of Language*. London: Routledge.

Wright, B.F. (1994). *The Real Mother Goose*. New York: Scholastic Inc.

Wykes, M., and Gunter, B. (2005). *The Media and Body Image*. Los Angeles: Sage Publications.

Zajko, V., and Leonard, M. (eds.). (2006). *Laughing With Medusa: Classical Myth and Feminist Thought*. New York: Oxford University Press.

ARTICLES IN JOURNALS

Albert, A.A., and Porter, J.R. (1988). Children's Gender-role Stereotypes: A Sociological Investigation of Psychological Models. *Sociological Forum*, 3(2), 184–210, doi: 10.1007/bf01115290

Anastasio, P.A., Rose, K.C., & Chapman, J. (1999). Can the Media Create Public Opinion? A Social-identity Approach. *Current Directions in Psychological Science*, 8(5), 152–155.

Baker-Sperry, L., and Grauerholz, L. (2003). The Pervasiveness and Persistence of the Feminine Beauty Ideal in Children's Fairy Tales. *Gender and Society*, 17(5), 711–726.

Bergvall, V.L. (1999). Toward a Comprehensive Theory of Language and Gender. *Language in Society*, 28(2), 273–293.

Carlson, S.M., and Marjorie, T. (2005). Imaginary Companions and Impersonated Characters: Sex Differences in Children's Fantasy Play. *Merrill Palmer Quarterly*, 51(1), 93–118.

Centre for Advocacy and Research. (2003). Contemporary Woman in Television Fiction: Deconstructing Role of 'Commerce' and 'Tradition'. *Economic and Political Weekly*, 38(17), 1684–1690, (26 Apr.–2 May 2003).

Ehrlich, S., and King, R. (1994). Feminist Meanings and the (de)Politici-
    zation of the Lexicon. *Language in Society*. 23(01), 59–76, doi:10.1017/
    S004740450001767X.
Fabes, R.A., Martin, C.L., and Hanish, L.D. (2004). The Next 50 Years:
    Considering Gender as a Context for Understanding Young Children's Peer
    Relationships. *Merrill-Palmer Quarterly*, 50(3), 260–273.
Hameed, Y. (ed.). (2007–8). 'Editorial' *Pakistani Literature*. Special issue,
    Women Writers, Vol. 12–13, 2007–8.
Hussein, J., (2004). A Cultural Representation of Women in the Oromo Society,
    African Study Monographs, 25(3), 103–147.
Hussein, J. (2005). The Social and Ethno-cultural Construction of Masculinity
    and Femininity in African Proverbs. *African Study Monographs*, 26(2): 59–87.
Kane, E.W. (2006). 'No Way My Boys Are Going to Be Like That!'. *Gender &
    Society*, 20(2), 149–176, doi: 10.1177/0891243205284276.
Katz, P. (1985). Toys to Grow On. *Feminist Teacher*, 1(4), University of Illinois
    Press.
Kothari, S. (2005). From Genre to Zanana: Urdu Television Drama Serials and
    Women's Culture in Pakistan. *Contemporary South Asia*, 14(3), 289–305.
Kuntjara. (2001). Beauty and the Beast: Images of Women in Advertisements.
    Nirvana, Vol. 3, No. 2, July 2001, pp. 97–106.
Lee, L. (2008). Understanding Gender through Disney's Marriages: A Study of
    Young Korean Immigrant Girls. *Early Childhood Education Journal*, 36(1),
    11–18, doi: 10.1007/s10643-008-0260-5.
Martin, C.L., Eisenbud, L., and Rose, H. (1995). Children's Gender-Based
    Reasoning about Toys. *Child Development*, 66(5), 1453–1471, doi: 10.1111/
    j.1467–8624.1995.tb00945.x
Martin, K.A., (1998). Becoming a Gendered Body: Practices of Preschools,
    American Sociological Review, 63(4), 494–511.
Mo, W., and Shen, W. (2002). The Women In and Behind the Rhymes. *Children's
    Literature in Education*. 33(2), 131–148, doi: 10.1023/a:1015283801417.
Network Women in Media. (2002). Women in Media. *Economic and Political
    Weekly*, Vol. 37(8), p. 804.
Sadik, N. (2001). Working towards Gender Equality in Marriage. *Innocenti
    Digest.*, No. 7, March 2001.
Stack, M., and Kelly, D.M. (2006). Popular Media, Education, and Resistance,
    Canadian Journal of Education/Revue canadienne de l'éducation, 29(1), 5–26.
Stoddart, T. and Turiel, E. (1985). Children's Concepts of Cross-Gender
    Activities. *Child Development*, 56(5), 1241–1252.
Storm, H. (1992). Women in Japanese Proverbs. *Asian Folklore Studies*, 51(2),
    167–182.

Tepper, C.A., and Cassidy, K.W. (1999). Gender Differences in Emotional Language in Children's Picture Books. *Sex Roles*, 40(3), 265–280. doi: 10.1023/a:1018803122469.

UNICEF Innocenti Research Centre. (2001). *Innocenti Digest*, No. 7, March 2001.

Wallowitz, L., (2004). Reading as Resistance: Gendered Messages in Literature and Media. *English Journal* 93(3), 26–31.

Weaver-Hightower, M. (2003). The 'Boy Turn' in Research on Gender and Education. *Review of Educational Research*. Vol. 73 (4), pp. 471–498.

Webster, S.K. (1982). Women, Sex, and Marriage in Moroccan Proverbs. *International Journal of Middle East Studies*. 14(2), 173–184.

Wohlwend, K. (2009). Damsels in Discourse: Girls Consuming and Producing Texts through Disney Princess Play. *Reading Research Quarterly*, 44(1), 57–83.

REPORT

Ministry of Education. (1959). Report of Commission on National Education. Islamabad: Government of Pakistan.

WEBSITES

Adeniyi, A. (2000). The Politics of Language. Retrieved 04/12/2008, www.raceandhistory.com/historicalviews/language.htm.

Beijing. (1985). Declaration and Platform for Action: A Guide for Women and Women's Groups, Retrieved 19/07/2011, www.bdix.net/sdnbd_org/world_env_day/2003/water.../beijing.pdf.

Diamantopoulou, A. (2002). Gender Equality and the Media. Retrieved 06/07/2011, www.publicservice.co.uk/feature_story.asp?id=358

Discourse, retrieved 04/12/2008, www.merriam-webster.com/dictionary/discourse.

Mohr, L., and Macharia, S. (2010). Who Makes the News? 2010 Global Monitoring Project. Retrieved 18/02/2011 www.genderlinks.org.za/attachment.php?aa_id=1233.

Musharraf, P. (speaker). (1999). Address to the Nation (written text) Musharraf, retrieved 4/11/2008, from www.chowk.com/articles/4656.

Robinson, L. (2004). 'Dirty' Discourse: The Politics of Gender Discourse in Popular Music. (Electronic version). *Mediations*, 1(1), retrieved 4/022008, www.fims.uwo.ca/mit/mediations/pdfs/Mediations-Essay06-Dirrty.pdf.

The Constitution of the Islamic Republic of Pakistan, Article 51(2), retrieved 17/12/2008, www.pakistani.org/pakistan/constitution.

Therapeutic Humor, IX(3), 1–2, Retrieved 04/12/2008, www.aath.org/articles/art_sultanoff01.html.

Index

A

Advertisements, 103–4, 107–9, 112, 162–8
Applied linguistics, 201

B

Binary division, 32–4, 116, 183

C

Coercive approach, 6, 9, 17
Communicative competence, 3
Connotation, 6, 19, 32–3, 43–4, 56, 86, 116, 172, 192, 194, 203
Control, 6, 8–9, 10–11, 13, 20–1, 24, 28, 49, 55, 120, 171, 187, 203
Critical discourse analysis, 12, 14, 58–9, 201

D

Deficit model of language, 53
Deviant, 30–2, 34, 38, 43, 52–3, 183, 192
Difference model of language, 55, 57
Dialect, 22, 56
Dialectical relation 4, 8, 197
Discourse, 3, 6–8, 11–15, 17–19, 25, 35–6, 52, 58–9, 62, 64–5, 76–7, 85, 121, 198–9, 200–1, 206
Discursive approach, 6, 9, 13, 17
Dominance model of language, 54–6
Dynamic approach, 59
Dynamics of power, 7, 14

E

ELT (English Language Teaching), 24, 199, 201–3, 205
English language, 3, 21, 23–4, 54–5, 196

F

Fairy tales, 125–6, 129, 132, 134, 138–9, 140, 141–9, 150–4
Feminist critique of language, 58
Feminist movement, 15
Film studies, 156–7, 161, 169, 173, 176–9, 180–4, 186–9, 203

G

Gender construction, 121, 138, 204
Gender ideology, 37
Gender trouble, 193
Ghazal, 68, 75

H

Hegemony, 6, 8–9, 17–18, 20–1, 49, 65, 120, 183, 199, 200–1, 203–4

I

Imperialism, 13, 21, 23, 176
India, 21–3, 69, 70, 100, 112–14, 117, 120, 137, 158–9, 165, 169, 173–80, 182–9, 202
Indo–Pak Subcontinent/Indian Subcontinent/Subcontinent/

United India, 3, 21–3, 66–7, 117–18, 122, 177, 182, 201,

J

Jokes, 53, 85–9, 91–9, 132, 179, 196, 203, 205

K

Knowledge and power, 10–13

L

Language, 2–7, 11–19, 20–4, 28, 30, 33, 36–8, 40, 45, 50, 52–9, 60, 63, 65, 67, 77, 79, 85–6, 91, 96, 98, 100, 103, 107, 124–5, 127, 153, 160, 162, 179, 181, 184, 189, 192–4, 196–9, 201–6
Language reform, 192–7
Langue, 2
Linguistic Imperialism, 13, 176
Lukes' dimensions of power, 9, 10
Manufacturing of consent, 17–18, 36, 168

M

Marginalized groups, 18, 36, 63–4, 79, 86, 98, 121
Matrimonial ads, , 103–14 Martians, 31
Media, 18, 20, 31, 36–7, 51, 62, 65, 84, 86, 100, 103, 114, 132, 156–61, 168, 170, 176–7, 181, 189, 196, 199, 202, 205–6
Melting Pot Approach, 21–2, 188
Mughal Empire, 3
Mushairas, 182

N

Nursery Rhymes/Rhymes, 125–37

O

Occident, 17
Orient, 17

P

Pakistan, 45, 63, 70, 107, 109, 110, 112–14, 118, 120, 158–60, 169, 170–3, 177, 182–5, 187, 189, 202
Patriarchy/patriarchal systems/ institutions, 30–1, 40, 47, 66, 100, 119, 122, 137, 147–8, 153, 172, 178, 183
Parole, 2
Persian, 3, 23, 179
Politics of language, 7, 14, 24, 198, 201
Politics of discourse, 8–15, 36–7, 58
Politics of representation, 17–20, 58, 85, 124, 140, 160, 184, 187, 192, 198–9, 201
Positional superiority, 17, 171

R

Resistance, 7, 11–12, 14, 102, 124, 152, 159, 198–9, 200–5

S

Sapir-Whorf hypothesis, 4–5, 11
Sayings and proverbs, 44, 77–84, 196, 203, 205
Sexism, 54–5, 194, 196
Social construct, 15, 46, 128, 138, 202, 206,
Social construction, 17–18, 59, 183
Social constructionist approach, 59

Social institutions, 6, 17–18, 30–1, 37, 46, 51, 62, 84, 86, 121, 138, 153, 156–7, 162, 193, 196, 199, 201–2, 206

Social reality, 5–6, 11–13, 24, 57, 79, 85–6, 124, 157, 162, 168, 192, 197–8

Socialization, 30, 37, 117, 144, 163, 168, 199

Songs, 36, 132, 176, 178–9, 181–9, 196, 203, 205

Spontaneous consent, 9, 10, 18, 122, 184

Sri Lanka, 113–14

Standard, 13, 19, 24, 31–2, 34, 38, 54, 63–4, 86, 171, 183–4, 188

T

Theatre, 169, 176–7, 179, 180
TV Plays, 157, 173, 203

U

Urdu Literature, 40, 66, 68–9, 70, 75–6
Urdu Parsee theatre, 176

V

Venusians, 31

INDEX OF NAMES

A

Ada Jaffery, 71, 75
Ahmed Rahi 187
Altaf Fatima, 70
Amjad Islam Amjad, 170–1
Ashfaq Ahmed, 170–1
Aishwarya Rai Bachchan, 180
Azra Abbas, 75

B

Baba Farid, 182
Bano Qudsia, 70, 170–1
Bulleh Shah, 182

D

Daniel Defoe, 23

E

Edward Said, 2, 85
Elaine Showalter, 203

F

Fatema Hasan, 75
Fatima Surria Bajia, 170–1
Fehmida Riaz, 71, 74–5,

G

Gulzar, 187

H

Hadiqa Kiani, 184
Hajra Masroor, 70
Haseena Moin, 170, 172
Helene Cixous, 76, 97
Hijab Imtiaz Ali, 69

I

Irfana Aziz, 75
Ismat Chughtai, 69, 70

J

Jacques Derrida, 203
Jagmohan, 180
Jamila Hashmi, 70
Jan Nisar Akhtar, 187

Javed Akhtar, 176–7
Jean Kilbourne, 162

K

Kabir, 182
Karl Marx, 62, 67
Khadija Mastoor, 70
Khalida Hussain, 70
Khushhal Khan Khattak, 182
Kishwar Naheed, 71–2, 75
Krishna Wamsi, 181
Kundan Shah, 181

M

Manish Jha, 180
Mansoora Ahmed, 75
Mian Muhammad, 182
Mumtaz Shireen, 70, 76

N

Naheed Qasmi, 75
Nasreen Anjum Bhatti, 75
Nazeer Ahmed, 67
Nilofer Iqbal, 70
Noor ul Huda Shah, 170, 172

P

Parveen Fana Syed, 75
Parveen Shakir, 75
Preity Zeinta, 181

Q

Qurratul Ain Hyder, 70

R

Raj Kumar Santoshi, 180
Ramesh Sippy, 178
Rasheed Jehan, 68–9
Rasheeda-tun- Nisa, 67
Razia Fasih Ahmed, 70
Riaz ur Rehman Saghar, 187
Robinson Crusoe, 23

S

Sahir Ludhianvi, 187
Samina Raja, 75
Sara Shagufta, 73, 75
Shabnam Shakeel, 75
Shah Hussain, 182
Shah Latif Bhitai, 182
Shaheen Mufti, 75
Shahid Nadeem, 172
Shahida Hasan, 75
Shaukat Siddiqui, 170
Sigmund Freud, 178

T

Tanveer Naqvi, 187

V

Vital Signs, 185

Z

Zahida Hina, 70
Zehra Nigah, 75
Ziaul Haq, 170–1